"This is the cookbook you won't be able to put down, can cook out of every day, and comes from the heart and soul of the stunningly talented Eden Grinshpan. Deciphering the flavors and techniques of the Levant? Sure. Delicious recipes? Absolutely. And this book does more than that, taking inspiration from Eden's childhood, where the kitchen was a safe place to express herself and passing that gift on to the readers and home cooks."
—ANDREW ZIMMERN, traveler, chef, writer, and teacher

"I have always said that my next culinary adventure would be to dive into the foods of the Middle East. Learning a new cuisine can be intimidating, but what I love about this book is that Eden gives you the basics of typical ingredients, sauces, and flavor combinations to get you started and then turns them on their head to provide her own modern and fresh approach that leaves you wanting to explore every dish in the book."
—MISSY ROBBINS, chef and owner of Lilia Ristorante and Misi; cofounder of Grovehouse

"*Eating Out Loud* is the kind of cookbook that you will actually use!! It will inspire you at the farmers market, get messy in your kitchen, and make you laugh on the couch. Eden has written a book about her life, which revolves around family, heritage, and glorious food. Bravo, dude."
—MICHAEL SOLOMONOV, chef of Zahav

"Eden is one of the most vivacious people in the food world and these recipes match her personality 100 percent. If you're looking for more flavor and fun in the kitchen, *Eating Out Loud* is your perfect guide."
—KERRY DIAMOND, founder of *Cherry Bombe* and author of *Cherry Bombe: The Cookbook*

"This book is a total party! These recipes are so colorful and vibrant that the flavors practically jump off of the page, right along with Eden's magnetic personality. If you're ever in need of a reason to get excited in the kitchen, just open up this book to literally any page."
—MOLLY YEH, TV host and author of *Molly on the Range*

Eating
Out Loud

Eating Out Loud

Bold Middle Eastern
Flavors for All Day,
Every Day

Eden Grinshpan

with Rachel Holtzman
Photographs by Aubrie Pick

Clarkson Potter/Publishers
New York

Library of Congress Cataloging-in-
Publication Data is available upon
request.

ISBN 978-0-593-13587-7
Ebook ISBN 978-0-593-13588-4

Printed in China

Book and cover design by Laura Palese
Photographs by Aubrie Pick

10 9 8 7 6 5 4 3 2 1

First Edition

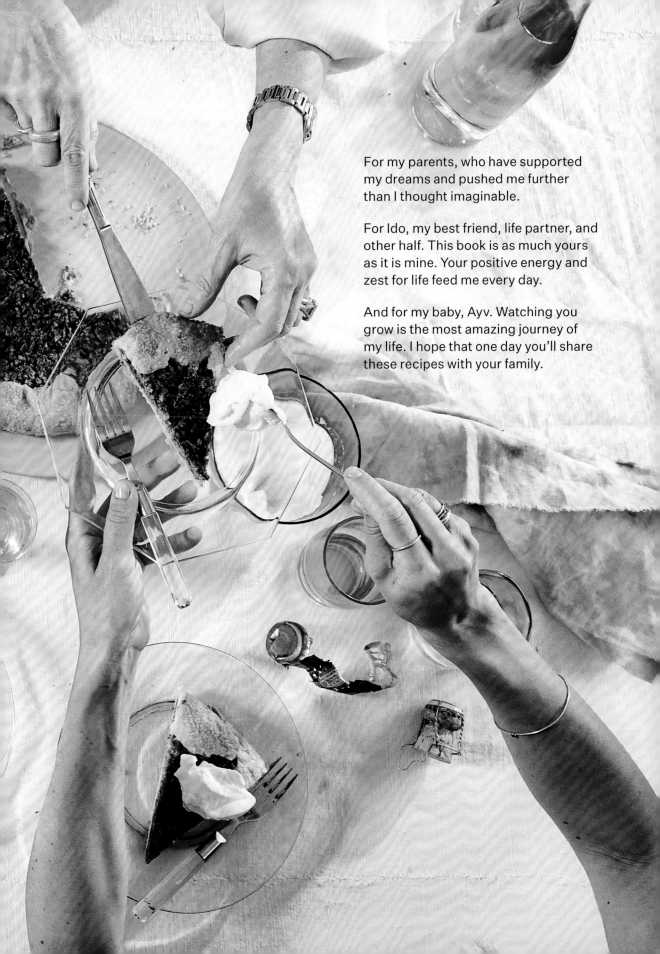

For my parents, who have supported my dreams and pushed me further than I thought imaginable.

For Ido, my best friend, life partner, and other half. This book is as much yours as it is mine. Your positive energy and zest for life feed me every day.

And for my baby, Ayv. Watching you grow is the most amazing journey of my life. I hope that one day you'll share these recipes with your family.

Contents

Growing up, I was lucky enough to eat dinner with my family almost every night.

Our ritual of sitting together never felt forced, and it was never just about sharing a meal. *Everything* happened at the dinner table—singing, laughing, crying, screaming, dancing—we're talking complete meshugas ("crazy" in Yiddish). It was a place for me and my two sisters to share our stories and to perform, whether it was impromptu Disney sing-alongs or crazy interpretive dance numbers. The three of us pushed one another to be as loud, obnoxious, and over-the-top as possible, and the kitchen table was our safe place to express ourselves.

And, of course, there was the food. In addition to being a total saint who put up with our constant nagging (*What's for dinnerrr??*), my mom had a handful of dishes that she did really well, like lemon-olive roast chicken or silky vegetable soups—whole foods cooked simply. (Just reading that sentence probably made her smile—Hi, Mom!) Then there were the nights when my dad would pick up something really special on his way home. We lived in Toronto, one of the most multicultural cities in the world, and we had the food to prove it. My dad loved introducing us to different flavors and delicacies from around the world, bringing home things like traditional Persian flatbreads, Turkish delight, and tongue sandwiches that most families I knew weren't sampling in their kitchens. For me,

eating these foods and experiencing all the diverse spices and ingredients that we'd be lucky to find in a run-of-the-mill grocery store (at least in 1990s Toronto) became a mission. So when I graduated from high school, I enrolled in Le Cordon Bleu in London.

It was a plan that sounded great in theory—it would be a way to learn some real skills, especially since no one I knew was looking to hire a professional lip-syncer, and I would get to cook while eating my way across Europe. But even though I fell madly in love with cooking, and at eighteen had no idea what else I was cut out to do, I knew that standing still in one place, working the same station at the same restaurant day in and day out, was not an option. All I wanted was to see the world, to chase all the flavors that my dad had introduced me to. And I wanted to share those stories! I knew firsthand how personal and connecting a meal could be, and I wanted to somehow re-create that with as many people as possible. I was always that girl getting all up in friends' faces about trying new foods ("You HAVE to try this!"), and I got such a high off being the person who introduced them to the best babka/baba ghanoush/Bolognese.

When I called my parents to tell them that I was going to spend the next year traveling instead of getting a "real" job, I thought they'd freak out. They didn't. Actually, the opposite. They encouraged me to go— just like they encouraged me to go to culinary school in the first place—and suggested that I bring along a camera to film the experience. (Are they not seriously the coolest?) Fast-forward two and a half years, and I had cooked, eaten, and lived in India, Southeast Asia, and Israel, soaking up every last aromatic rice dish, spicy braised stew, vibrant vegetable curry, dumplings, noodles, and pita everything. I volunteered with local organizations, tapped in to communities and their unique stories, and learned about the food cultures that tied it all together. It turned out my parents were right about what a smart move this was for me, and about filming it—I transformed that footage into a reel and ended up with dream jobs hosting shows like *Eden Eats* and *Log On & Eat with Eden Grinshpan* for Cooking Channel, and *Top Chef Canada*. And all that cooking experience made it possible for me to eventually open my very own restaurant, DEZ, in New York City.

But it was the last stop on my whirlwind *Eat, Pray, Love* tour that totally changed my life.

I'm half Israeli and grew up visiting Israel every summer. But this trip was completely different—having just finished culinary school, it was like meeting the country for the first time. I had a better understanding of the food, how it was made, and where the ingredients came from. And I asked a lot more questions. I wanted to know everything about this crazy mishmash of flavors that drew from places in North Africa, the Middle East, the Mediterranean, and about a million years of culinary history. I had things like *jachnun*, a flaky, doughy Yemeni bread; *sabich*, pita stuffed with fried eggplant, spicy pickled mango, and Chopped Salad (the holy trinity of cucumbers, tomatoes, and fresh herbs); and *baladi*, a fat wild eggplant that's burnt to a crisp so the insides get custardy and smoky, then drizzled with toppings like tangy pomegranate molasses or nutty tahini. I learned that the universal cooking fat is extra-virgin olive oil (no dish is complete without a generous cascade of a bright, fruity varietal), and that there's no wrong time in the day for eggs, especially if they're poached in a spiced tomato-pepper sauce and sopped up with pita, à la shakshuka. I fell in love with zesty, bright sumac; the briny tang of sheep's milk feta; and the surprisingly tart but balanced punch that pomegranate molasses adds to richly flavored dishes. And I met my mate for life: tahini. We're talking an epic obsession. I couldn't get enough of the rich, creamy sesame paste that is essentially the Israeli

mother sauce. In Israel, I found it dolloped onto roasted vegetable and fish dishes, whisked into spreads, shaken into dressings, and added to pretty much everything that hit the table, sweet or savory. Now I barely put out anything without a drizzle of the stuff, and let me tell you, just about everything is better for it. I'm a firm believer in the motto "If you fuck it up, put tahini on it." I'd like to think if Julia Child were Israeli, she would have said the same thing.

Ultimately, I learned how to take a small collection of simple and traditional ingredients, mix and match them in new, fresh ways, and create dishes perfect for dunking, picking, dipping, dribbling, schmearing, and getting all up in with your hands. When I changed the way I cooked, I suddenly started having much more fun in the kitchen. I didn't dread the question "What's for dinner?"—a question that my husband, Ido (obviously an Israeli husband with a name like Ido . . . what can I say, I love the men as much as I love the food), and I start asking each other around 10 a.m. every single day. Best of all, I *always* had something easy to make and tasty to eat, whether it was for my husband and three-year-old daughter Ayv, a hot date night (on the couch, obvi), a last-minute get-together with friends, a special gathering or holiday, or a stuff-it-all-in-my-mouth-one-handed situation while doing errands with the stroller or pumping. This is food for *real life*—feeding yourself, feeding your family, and feeding the people whom you care about most; no big, annoying shopping lists, real pants, or silverware required. That's what *Eating Out Loud* is all about.

But enough about me. . . . This is why you're going to love this book:

I'm going to introduce you to your new Middle Eastern pantry—ingredients that take even the simplest plate of roasted vegetables or bowl of grains to the next level. From za'atar and preserved lemon to sesame seeds and turmeric-pickled cauliflower, I'll show you how a truly great meal is just a matter of throwing a bunch of these tasty things on a plate or in a bowl. Seriously! These classic ingredients have been simplified, mashed up, and riffed on and since they grew up together, they get along really well and hit all the right notes—creamy and rich, bright and tart, crunchy and nutty, salty and briny, earthy and floral. I'll also show you some of my favorite recipes for essentials: a collection of spreads, condiments, dressings, toppers, spice mixes, and other easy add-ins that bring together seemingly random ingredients to make an instant meal. For example, my ride-or-die tahini sauces (pages 37 to 38); labneh (page 52), which is ridiculously thick, tangy yumminess that's just strained yogurt; and spice-infused pickles (page 57). I'll include some of my favorite traditional recipes, like *chraime* (page 194), fish bathed in a spicy, cumin-scented tomato sauce; *siniya* (page 217), and ground lamb baked in tahini Palestinian-style. And then there will be my updated twists, like Epic Seedy Granola (page 91), Turmeric–Black Pepper Malawach (page 145), and Sesame Challah Monkey Bread (page 92).

I promise you this is so *not* the cookbook that will talk a big game about your new "simple" pantry, then ask you to get one thousand new ingredients for each recipe. I've been there; it sucks. And yes, I went to culinary school, but none of that fancy business has any place in your kitchen. Instead, I'll teach you my "Best Of" tricks, like roasting vegetables until they're just about burnt (oh hello, smoky, caramelized veggies), taking seemingly savory ingredients and turning them into the most incredible desserts— check out Yogurt and Sour Cream Cheesecake (page 247)—and making the perfect Pickled, Herby, Charred Peppers (page 55), which you can always have a batch of in the fridge to toss into pita, grain bowls, or salads. I'll give you recipes for any time of day or occasion, from breakfast for real people (because let's be honest, no one's cooking *anything* on a Monday morning) to Eggs All Day (very Israeli, very delicious), easily whipped-up bowls to handheld

A Shout-Out to My Kosher Krew

These recipes are influenced by my experiences in Israel, my travels, and my Jewish background, but some do still call for a few *treif*-y things (such as shellfish or pork) and the occasional mingling of meat and dairy. No worries—I got you! All the accompaniments work just as well with other proteins, like fish, chicken, or kosher steak, and you can simply omit the dairy where needed. You'll still end up with an incredible dish.

meals, bigger-deal dinners (a step up from things in pita, but no fussier) to sweets infused with Middle Eastern flavors: Salted Halvah Chocolate Chip Cookies (page 245). Boom.

And I'll also give you tips for how to feed a crowd. Filling my home with people is as nourishing to me as food itself. It's something my husband and I make a point of doing regularly, whether it's opening our doors on a Sunday for anyone who wants to come by or hosting special holiday meals. (Okay, maybe not as much when we were baby-feeding/changing/rocking zombies, which is when takeout and paper plates were *completely* in order. . . .) No matter how "nice" the meal is, though, I can still relax and have a good time because I know that all of these recipes that I've collected and honed are easy to make and that these dishes can go straight out to the table from the oven or stove looking just as sexy as if I had taken the time to arrange things on a platter. (And that the Fleetwood Mac Spotify station is just as important an ingredient as salt and pepper, but that's another story.) Plus, these flavors speak of a place and a vibe that's home to me. Food that is warm and welcoming like that makes everyone else feel good, too. When I look around the table and see a collection of double-dipping, hand-eating, pants-unbuttoning guests, I know it's been a successful night. That is the spirit that I fell in love with while living in Israel, and it's what's at the heart of *Eating Out Loud*.

Your New Middle Eastern Pantry

These are the secret weapons that add that extra pop of flavor to everything I cook, taking super-simple dishes to the next level of complexity and deliciousness.

As I ate my way across Israel and many Mediterranean countries, I collected a solid rotation of spices, seeds, herbs, and other staple ingredients that I'm pretty much always reaching for. Don't worry, though—we're not gonna go nuts here. Your pantry is something that you can build over time, and because you'll be cooking from this book, it'll happen naturally. You'll see that I call for these ingredients over and over again—namely because they're all (a) amazing, (b) versatile, and (c) take on a whole range of flavors depending on how you're using them. And the best part is that you can now find most of these things in your local grocery store, or at the very least on Amazon.

Aleppo pepper

This is a variety of chile pepper from Syria that's used primarily in Middle Eastern cuisine. I love finishing dishes with it—veggies, eggs, fish, whatevs—because it adds a mellow back-of-the-tongue heat that's not too overpowering while also bringing some citrusy brightness. And the best part is that as it warms up, its oils release their gorgeous red color, which runs out on the plate and begs for sopping up with some pita.

Amba
(pickled mango sauce)

It can be hard to describe the flavor of this sauce, which is originally from Iraq but is now used in Israeli cuisine, primarily as the magic ingredient that takes pita sandwiches to the next level. It packs major tangy brightness, and I promise once you try it, you won't be able to get enough of it. You can find this condiment in most Middle Eastern markets, and Trader Joe's recently started carrying it, too. In my opinion, some things are just better store-bought—and that includes amba.

Baharat

Arabic for "spice," baharat is basically an all-purpose blend that covers your ass in the flavor department. It's a one-and-done kinda deal with warm and savory notes from spices like cumin, cinnamon, coriander, and cloves. Each region has its own variation, so I highly recommend finding a version that you love.

If you can't find this at the store, just mix together ¼ cup toasted coriander seeds, ground; 2 tablespoons toasted cumin seeds, ground; 1 teaspoon ground cinnamon; 2 teaspoons ground cloves; 2 teaspoons ground black peppercorns; ½ teaspoon ground cardamom; and 2 teaspoons ground nutmeg. Store in an airtight container for up to 6 months.

Cardamom

I had my first love affair with cardamom when I was backpacking in India thirteen years ago and learned that it was the secret ingredient in the chai that I couldn't get enough of. Then I found out that it was also the floral note in Turkish coffee that I loved so much. It has a warm and slightly sweet essence, and it's downright magical when added to baked goods. Seriously, any excuse I have to bake with it, I'm there. Cardamom in its whole form comes in a pod, which you have to crack open to get the seeds and then grind. Be good to yourself and just buy it already ground.

Coriander seeds

I find myself going back to coriander again and again because of its deep, earthy flavor that has just a hint of citrus. It's great for tossing whole into pickling brines and braises, and toasting and grinding for building sauces, soups, and stews. You can buy ground coriander, but I recommend skipping it in favor of toasting and grinding the whole seeds yourself—you'll get a much richer product with *so* much more flavor.

Couscous

This reminds me of my childhood, when we'd spend the day at the beach and my parents would order us couscous with a sweet vegetable stew poured on top for dinner. You'd never know if the tiny bits were couscous or sand, but it didn't really matter because it was just that good. Couscous is like a little Middle Eastern pasta that's made from semolina, and it's one of those go-to bases that you can season however you like. You could go savory with meat or veg, or sweet with brown butter, dried fruits, and spices. Even though the true traditional cooking method for couscous is a lot more involved than just adding boiling water or stock—which is all you need to do when you buy it at most Western supermarkets—I'm all about making my life—and yours—easier. Just buy the stuff at the store!

Cracked freekeh

"Freaky," as they call it in Israel, is durum wheat that's picked while it's still green, then sun-dried and roasted. I've recently added it to the rotation and cannot get sick of it. It's super nutty and has incredible texture with a great bite, which is perfect for using as the base of different salads and stews, or stuffed into tomatoes or peppers. "Cracked" just means that the whole grain has been crushed into pieces, which makes it cook more quickly. I love making a big batch and keeping it in the fridge during the week so all I need to do for a quick meal is toss in some Garlicky Tahini (page 37) or a Seven-Minute Egg (page 52) and maybe some leftover veggies.

Cumin seeds

Cumin is one of those strong, earthy spices that people are really opinionated about—you either love it or hate it. But I think it comes down to how you use it—you want to add just enough that you get all its rich, toasty flavor but not so much that it's all you taste. Like most other whole-seed spices, I strongly urge you to toast and grind cumin yourself; its flavor is so much more powerful than preground. I promise I'll give you plenty of other shortcuts, but not this one.

Extra-virgin olive oil

This is my favorite fat to cook with and also to drizzle over just about everything before serving it. You want to spend a little more here—it's the difference between something generic and flavorless (that's a big no) and one that's exceptional. There's a huge range of qualities in olive oils, and while I like to stay in the Mediterranean family, go with what makes you happy, whether it's spicy, fruity, grassy, etc. It's going to make your dishes that much better. That said, I save the really good stuff for dressings and finishing off a dish with a drizzle. For cooking, you can go with an extra-virgin oil that's more middle-of-the-road in terms of fancy factor.

Fresh herbs

Most people know that sprinkling fresh green herbs like parsley, mint, dill, cilantro, or basil over a dish is the quickest way to give it a colorful, vibrant look. But the reason I use them by the handful is because of the flavor and aroma they add. Embracing the true, natural plant-ness of the herbs is a real game changer that just elevates all of the other flavors on a plate. Play around to see which herbs speak to you—they all have different personalities—and don't be shy when adding them to a dish. I particularly love scattering them in salads in an almost equal proportion to the greens.

Fresh lemon

It's such a simple no-brainer—a squeeze of lemon juice brings beautiful brightness and acidity to pretty much anything you'll cook. Acid is something you hear about all the time when it comes to making a well-rounded dish, and that's because it adds a fresh, clean note that lets all the other flavors come forward that much more—similar to adding salt. Fresh lemon is a ridiculously easy way to do just that.

Nigella seeds

The first time I had these gorgeous black seeds was on a Persian flatbread from a bakery that my dad would take me to in Toronto. Like cumin, these seeds have an earthiness but with a nuttiness and a slight taste of onions. After tasting them baked into bread, I had to go and buy some for myself so I could play around with them in my cooking. Now I love sprinkling them over a dish for their texture and flavor, which I bring out even more by toasting the seeds first.

Paprika

Whether you're using sweet or smoky, there are very few things that don't get better with the bold depth of flavor paprika adds. I guarantee that your life will get better once you add this to your spice lineup.

Pomegranate molasses

This is one of those sneaky ingredients that gives a little extra something to a dish, but people can never figure out what it is. It's essentially pomegranate juice that's been reduced until it's sticky and sour and sweet, and it adds depth and brightness to just about anything, whether it's a deep, smoky eggplant dish or a light freekeh salad. It can be a little bit of a balancing act to use because of its natural sour flavor, which is why less is more.

Seeds

The smell of toasting seeds—whether sunflower, sesame, or pumpkin—reminds me of walking the streets of Israel in the hot, hot summer with my family, eating bags and bags of roasted sunflower seeds until our lips would blister and crack from the salt. We'd eat handfuls of the toasty, crunchy nuttiness, then wash 'em down with huge bottles of water. In my kitchen, I love toasting seeds until they release their nutty-flavored oils, then using them as a topping for adding beautiful depth of flavor and crunchy texture.

Sheep's milk feta

Crumbling this tangy, briny cheese over a dish adds instant creaminess and body plus a salty kick that brings out all of the other flavors. I prefer sheep's milk because it has a creamier texture than other fetas out there, and I specifically love Bulgarian feta because it's really popular in Israel. If you can't find it, any other feta you can get your hands on is fine. But I guarantee that once you try sheep's milk, you'll never go back.

Sumac

This spice actually comes from a berry, which grows wild in the Mediterranean and Middle East. It has an incredibly bright flavor, like a super citrus, which is why I love using it to finish salads or grilled meat and fish dishes—along with its beautifully deep purple-red color.

Tahini

I have a serious crush on tahini—and it can get a
little intense. Any excuse to use it, and I am GAME.
Tahini—or if you want to sound legit, *t'hina* (the "t"
and "h" make a sound like you're hardcore clearing
your throat so the word comes out more like *trina*)—is
a rich, creamy, toasty, nutty sesame seed paste. Along
with chickpeas, it's the base of hummus—so unless
you haven't had hummus before, you've all had tahini.
A lot of the dishes that you'll find in this book include
tahini, and if they don't, there's still a good chance
that they would be just as awesome (or even more
awesome) with tahini included. It's pretty much the
perfect condiment—it adds so much gorgeous richness
to a dish, and it helps bring all the flavors into balance
in a way that no other ingredient can. It rounds out
bitterness, balances brighter acidic notes, and doesn't
overwhelm subtler ingredients, yet can still hold its
own with big, bold ones. You can drizzle it straight from
the jar to finish a dish or whisk it with garlic, lemon
juice, and water for more of a dressing or sauce; it's the
perfect base for a spread; and you can enjoy it in savory
and sweet dishes (seriously, just mix in a little honey
and spread it on some fresh bread . . . it's f'n good). Can
you see why I'm obsessed?

When buying a tahini paste, you want to look at
where the sesame seeds are from and how they're
processed. The best tahinis are made with sesame
seeds from Humera in Ethiopia. When you buy the jars,
the oil usually separates and rises to the top. If you
shake it and it combines easily, that's usually a sign
of good-quality tahini. If it doesn't mix, it won't be as
great. I personally also buy the lighter color tahini. I
think it has a sweeter, nuttier flavor, while the darker
ones are a little more bitter.

Turmeric

Yes, it's trendy; yes, it has major antioxidant and anti-inflammatory health benefits; and yes, it belongs in your kitchen on the regular. I've been using ground turmeric as the base of my cooking for years because I love how its natural earthiness grounds a dish (and probably because subconsciously I knew how good it is for you). Plus, its deep golden color is like sunshine on a plate, and who doesn't like eating happy food? You'll want to go easy with this one—too much can be extremely bitter and medicinal tasting.

Urfa

This is a Turkish spice that I started playing with more recently, and now I'm full-on obsessed. It's a dried pepper with a deep, raisin-like sweetness and a warm, subtle heat. I kinda go nuts sprinkling it on anything and everything—roasted tomatoes with olive oil and honey, crispy potatoes, grilled fish or meat. Basically, any time you're reaching for red chile flakes, grab these instead.

Za'atar

This blend, for me, is the true essence of Middle Eastern spices. Its signature combination of wild oregano, sumac, sesame seeds, and salt always calls to mind my time growing up in Israel, going to the markets in Tel Aviv, and eating za'atar-dusted bread fresh out of the oven. It's incredibly savory and versatile, so it pairs well with just about everything. Slathering it over chicken before it roasts is a classic, or you can do what I do and mix it with extra-virgin olive oil and drizzle it over everything—including fresh-baked bread and roasted veg.

If you can't find earthy wild oregano at the store, you can pretty closely mimic it by blending ¼ cup fresh thyme leaves and 2 tablespoons dried oregano, then mixing in a heaping 2 tablespoons sumac, ⅓ cup toasted sesame seeds, and ½ teaspoon kosher salt for homemade za'atar. Store in an airtight container for several months.

NOTE ON KOSHER SALT *I used Diamond Crystal when testing the recipes in the book. Since different brands of salt can vary in sodium content, always remember to taste as you go.*

The Essentials

When I tell you that these sauces and dips are essentials, I really do mean it.

As in, necessities. They're the go-tos that are pretty much always in my fridge, help make almost any dish more interesting and fresher, and are super clutch when I need to just throw something together to eat in minutes. These are the versatile basics that will make the recipes in this book more delicious, and many are perfect in their own right. If I'm having people over, I'm always going to begin with a bunch of mezze, or small starter salads and dips—along with tons of pita or flatbreads, which is a pretty standard Middle Eastern move. When you go out to eat in Israel, they usually serve a platter of mezze and you have at it. And if you're still hungry for a kebab afterward, it's honestly impressive. I like to take the same approach, whether I'm just feeding Ido and Ayv or I'm packing a crowd into our apartment. I love going into the fridge and grabbing all the different jars and quart containers I've collected—creamy tahini sauces, spicy spreads, all kinds of pickles—and putting them together like a little smorgasbord. All that's left to do is throw together a quick one-pan meal, make a fresh salad or two, and warm up some pita or flatbread, then we all just get in there with our hands and dip, schmear, and assemble. Half the time we don't even make it to the table because we're too busy picking straight from the pan.

Garlicky Tahini

Makes about 2 cups

Something magical happens when you blend tahini paste with ice water: It transforms into a rich and creamy sauce or dressing (shout-out to Mike Solomonov for this ice water hack; I swear it makes the sauce that much lighter and more velvety in texture). Add a hit of garlic, lemon juice, and salt and you'll instantly have the Swiss Army knife of condiments in your fridge that you can use to finish just about any dish—fish, meat, grains, roasted veggies, salads, or sandwiches. It's also perfect for using as the foundation for hummus. Garlicky Tahini also happens to be how I sneak protein into any vegetable meal. I'm an addict, and now Ayv is, too.

1 cup tahini paste

2 teaspoons fresh lemon juice, plus more to taste

1 garlic clove, grated

1 teaspoon kosher salt, plus more to taste

½ cup ice water, plus more if needed (see Note)

NOTE *This is how much I need for the brand of tahini that I use, but it may be different for you. Start with some of the water and add until you've gotten a smooth, creamy consistency. If you add too much water, add a little more tahini to thicken the sauce back up again.*

In a medium bowl, whisk together the tahini, lemon juice, garlic, salt, and ice water. It will reach a weird, lumpy consistency, but don't be afraid. Keep whisking until it smooths out and becomes light in color (if it doesn't, it needs more ice water, so just add a bit more). Tahini sauce with the perfect consistency will drip through the tines of a fork, but just barely. Taste for seasoning, adding more lemon juice or salt if desired. Store in a jar in the fridge for up to 1 week. If the tahini gets too thick while in the fridge, just loosen it up with a little water before using.

VARIATION

Green Tahini

Classic Garlicky Tahini is perfect for slathering over anything and everything, but this version takes it to an even fresher, brighter place. I went for crisp green parsley, but you could also try dill or chives for even bolder flavor. I love using this on salad, eggs, and grilled fish. **Makes about 2 cups**

1 recipe Garlicky Tahini

½ cup packed fresh flat-leaf parsley leaves, dill, or chives (or a blend of all 3)

Ice water (optional)

Make the garlicky tahini as directed above. Transfer to a blender or food processor, add the herbs, and blend until smooth. If the sauce gets too thick while blending, add ice water 1 tablespoon at a time until it gets nice and drizzly. Store in a jar in the fridge for up to 5 days.

Charred Tahini

Makes about 3 cups

One of the best discoveries I made while traveling through Israel is the genius way that smoky burnt skin from charred eggplant is used to make charred tahini. Instead of throwing it away, you can blend it with tahini, whose nutty creaminess balances out any bitterness.

1 recipe Garlicky Tahini (page 37)

1 cup charred eggplant skin (see Note)

In a blender or food processor, combine the garlicky tahini and eggplant skin and blend until smooth. Store in a jar in the fridge for up to 1 week.

NOTE *Save the eggplant skin from either of these two recipes: Baba Ghanoush with Za'atar, Pomegranate, and Mint (page 42) or Charred Whole Eggplant with Crushed Tomatoes, Basil, and Mint (page 181).*

Classic Hummus

Makes about 6 cups

I—literally—couldn't write a book about Middle Eastern food without talking about hummus. Even though it's such a simple dip to make, everyone has their own unique preferences and tips. For me, it's all about a really creamy, tahini-heavy hummus that's a lot lighter than people are used to in the States. In Israel, you go to a hummus spot and an order of hummus is your meal. That would be impossible with the denser, gloopier hummus that you're used to seeing here, especially the store-bought stuff. So selfishly, I love this version because it means I can eat it by the tubful. The trick is incorporating more tahini than you'd think, plus a lot of ice water.

Hummus

3 cups cooked or canned chickpeas (about two 15.5-ounce cans), rinsed and drained (see Note)

1 cup ice water

1 cup tahini paste

2 tablespoons fresh lemon juice

2½ teaspoons kosher salt

1 garlic clove

Tahini Sauce (optional for extra creamy texture)

¼ cup tahini paste

¼ teaspoon kosher salt

Serving

Hummus Vinaigrette (recipe follows) or 1 lemon and extra-virgin olive oil

Paprika (you could also use za'atar or Aleppo pepper)

Zhug, Red and Green (optional; page 50)

Pickles (optional)

Pitas (optional), homemade (see page 150) or store-bought (also amazing with challah)

1 Make the hummus: In a blender or food processor (the more high-powered your blender, the fluffier your hummus will be), combine the chickpeas, ice water, tahini, lemon juice, salt, and garlic and blend until smooth. (If making ahead, you can store the hummus in a jar in the fridge for up to 1 week.)

2 Make the tahini sauce: In a medium bowl, stir together the tahini, salt, and ¼ cup plus 1 tablespoon water until smooth.

3 To serve: Spread the hummus on a plate. Add a drizzle of the tahini sauce in the center, followed by a drizzle of the hummus vinaigrette (or the lazy version—a squeeze of lemon juice and a drizzle of olive oil), then a good pinch of paprika. If desired, serve zhug, pickles, and pita alongside.

NOTE ON CHICKPEAS
I get that when you buy a cookbook, you want THE BEST recipes for everything, especially the kinds of staples that you want to make all the time. And yes, if I were cooking in a restaurant, I'd be cooking chickpeas from scratch. But when I'm at home? Nope. Not gonna happen because (a) who has time? and (b) I don't think it makes that big of a difference. So if you want to use canned, no judgment! If you can get food on the table AND it's delicious, then major kudos to you. And if you want to cook chickpeas yourself? Go for it—just start with 1½ cups dried chickpeas soaked overnight with 1 teaspoon of baking soda and water. The next day, drain and cook in simmering water until tender enough that they easily come apart when pinched.

HUMMUS VINAIGRETTE

Makes about ½ cup

In Israel, this bright vin is called *tatbila* and is served over hummus to help cut through the richness. Adding chile pepper is traditional, and I love the heat it adds, but it's not mandatory—feel free to leave it out. This recipe makes enough for about 4 servings' worth of hummus, but you can easily scale up.

½ long hot pepper, finely chopped (optional)
¼ cup extra-virgin olive oil
2 tablespoons fresh lemon juice
½ garlic clove, grated
Pinch of kosher salt

In a medium bowl, whisk together the hot pepper (if using), olive oil, lemon juice, garlic, and salt.

Baba Ghanoush with Za'atar, Pomegranate, and Mint

Makes about 4 cups

What makes this an essential is the eggplant technique, which is so simple but blows your mind at the same time. I learned about charring eggplants whole when I was twenty-one years old and working in a restaurant in Tel Aviv. They'd score an eggplant, throw the entire thing on the grill, and then let the fire do all the work. The skin gets completely charred while the heat steams the flesh until it is smoky, tender, and juicy. That becomes the foundation of baba ghanoush, a smoky, velvety dip that's an essential in its own right.

3 medium eggplants

½ cup tahini paste

2 tablespoons fresh lemon juice

1 garlic clove, grated

1½ teaspoons kosher salt

Za'atar, for serving

Extra-virgin olive oil, for serving

Pomegranate molasses, for serving

Fresh mint leaves, for serving

Pomegranate seeds, for serving (if in season)

1   With the tip of a knife, pierce each eggplant in two places—doesn't need to be perfect or in the same place every time; this is just so the eggplant doesn't explode on you (it's happened to me, and it's not pretty).

2   **Pick a cooking method for the eggplant:** grill, broiler, or stovetop burners. The bottom line is that you want this eggplant to be almost unrecognizable. It's going to deflate and the skin will get white in some places, but that just means the fire is working its magic on that eggplant.

OPTION 1: Grill Preheat the grill until hot. Add the eggplants and let the fire do its thing, making sure to keep turning the eggplants so they char all over. You want them to get black in some places, 20 to 30 minutes total.

OPTION 2: Broil Preheat the broiler. Put the eggplants in a broilerproof roasting pan and place the pan as close to the heating element as possible. (You may have to adjust your oven rack to accommodate the size of the eggplants and the depth of the pan.) Broil until they are evenly charred all over, 30 to 35 minutes, checking and turning the eggplants periodically. You want the eggplants to keep their shape but get really charred and wilted.

OPTION 3: Stovetop Gas Burners Line your stovetop around your burners with foil. Working with one at a time, place the eggplant over a medium flame and let it char, making sure to turn it every 5 minutes. Continue cooking until it is deflated and black all over, 20 to 30 minutes.

3 Transfer the cooked eggplants to a colander in the sink and let the juices run. (The juices can make the dish taste bitter.) Once the eggplants are cool enough to handle, remove the stem and all of the skin. (Feel free to reserve the skin to make Charred Tahini, page 38.)

4 In a medium bowl, whisk together the eggplant flesh with the tahini, lemon juice, garlic, and salt.

5 To serve, first make a za'atar oil by mixing together 1 tablespoon of za'atar with 1½ tablespoons of olive oil for every 2 cups of baba ghanoush.

6 For each serving, use a spoon to spread about 1 cup of the baba ghanoush over a platter or in the bottom of a bowl. Drizzle over 1 to 2 teaspoons of the pomegranate molasses (go easy—it's very tart and sweet), followed by the za'atar–olive oil mixture. Finish with a sprinkling of small mint leaves (or large leaves, torn) and a small handful of pomegranate seeds (if using).

Spicy Tomato and Red Pepper Matbucha

Serves 4 as a dip

Matbucha (mat-boo-ha) means "cooked salad" in Arabic, and it's a tomato-y, pepper-y acidic dip or spread that can be used tons of different ways. Traditionally, you see it on mezze platters—super important, since it balances out the creamier, richer classics like hummus and baba—or as a side. In our house, though, it's an all-purpose condiment that's just as perfect for dolloping on grain salads, spreading on sandwiches, or serving over eggs.

3 tablespoons extra-virgin olive oil

4 red bell peppers, diced

1 large yellow onion, diced

2 heaping teaspoons Aleppo pepper or red chile flakes, plus more (optional) for serving

2 teaspoons sweet paprika

1 teaspoon smoked paprika

2 teaspoons kosher salt, plus more to taste

½ teaspoon freshly ground black pepper

3 garlic cloves, minced

1 tablespoon red wine vinegar

6 medium tomatoes (see Note), chopped

1 teaspoon sugar

NOTE *When I call for tomatoes, I mean the best, freshest, juiciest, sweetest tomatoes you can find. In the summer, tomatoes on the vine, Roma, or heirlooms are the way to go. Otherwise, I use canned San Marzanos.*

1   In a large skillet, heat the olive oil over medium heat. Add the bell peppers, onion, Aleppo pepper, sweet paprika, smoked paprika, salt, and black pepper. Cook until the vegetables are tender, 7 to 10 minutes. Add the garlic and cook for another minute. Add the vinegar and use your spoon to scrape up all the browned bits from the bottom of the pan.

2   Stir in the tomatoes and sugar and check for seasoning. Add a pinch more salt if it needs it—it should be tangy and sweet. Let the mixture reduce over medium-low heat until it's a thick, sweet, sticky sauce and the tomatoes have completely broken down, about 40 minutes. Let the mixture cool slightly before serving with a sprinkle of Aleppo (if desired), or let it cool completely and store in a jar in the fridge for up to 1 week.

Chermoula

Makes about 1 cup

Everyone should have a go-to chermoula, a pungent Moroccan preserved lemon, fresh herb, and spice relish, and this is mine. I love how it infuses meat, fish, and even vegetables with bright, layered flavor. Just make sure to toast your spices first to release all of their lovely oils.

2 teaspoons coriander seeds, toasted in a dry pan until fragrant

2 teaspoons cumin seeds, toasted in a dry pan until fragrant

1 preserved lemon, store-bought or homemade (page 53)

1 cup fresh flat-leaf parsley leaves

¾ cup extra-virgin olive oil

4 garlic cloves, peeled but left whole

2 teaspoons Aleppo pepper or red chile flakes

1 teaspoon sweet paprika

1 teaspoon kosher salt

½ teaspoon ground turmeric

1   Using a spice grinder or mortar and pestle, grind the coriander and cumin. (You could also buy ground spices if you need to.)

2   Rinse the preserved lemon. Scrape off and discard the pulp. Transfer the peel to a blender or food processor. Add the coriander, cumin, parsley, oil, garlic, Aleppo pepper, paprika, salt, and turmeric and blend until combined but still a little chunky. Store in a jar in the fridge for up to 1 week.

Harissa

Makes about 2 cups

I love making my own hot sauces, including Zhug (page 50) and this peppery Moroccan number. It's super simple to do and makes people feel really special when you're serving it. (And it doesn't hurt that it's totally impressive, too.) Whenever I put out a spread, I always include a little dish of harissa on the side so people can mix and dip as they like. This beautiful combo of toasted chiles, spices, and garlic doesn't give you a ton of heat, just lots of deep, smoky flavor and a gorgeous red color. A drizzle of the oil that separates from the solids is also the perfect way to finish a dish.

15 dried guajillo or pulla chiles

1 cup grapeseed oil

3 tablespoons distilled white vinegar

2 fresh cayenne or bird's-eye chiles or other hot red chile

2 large garlic cloves, peeled but left whole

2 teaspoons cumin seeds, toasted in a dry pan until fragrant

2 teaspoons coriander seeds, toasted in a dry pan until fragrant

2 teaspoons sweet paprika

2 teaspoons kosher salt

¼ teaspoon smoked paprika

1   Bring a large pot of water to a boil. Add the dried chiles, reduce the heat to medium-low, and gently simmer for 20 minutes to rehydrate the chiles. Drain and when cool enough to handle, remove and toss the stems. Drain any water that may be left inside the chiles.

2   In a blender or food processor, combine the rehydrated chiles with the oil, vinegar, cayenne chiles, garlic, cumin, coriander, sweet paprika, salt, and smoked paprika and blend until the mixture forms a smooth paste. I like how the oil separates, but if you want a more spreadable condiment, emulsify it with a tablespoon or two of water. The more water you add, the creamier it becomes. Store in a jar in the fridge for 1 month (though mine always lasts longer).

Sunchoke Hummus

Makes about 3 cups

Sunchokes add such a unique, almost nutty, artichoke-like flavor. They are one of Ido's all-time favorite vegetables, and one of the best parts of working with them is that Ido thinks I've done so much work developing flavors in a dish, but the truth is, I'm just using sunchokes, which add their own complexity. Throw in a little lemon and garlic, and it takes the ingredient to a whole new place. Ido actually gave me the idea of adding sunchokes to hummus, and once we tried it, it was Game Over. The sunchokes not only puree beautifully, but they're also a natural pairing with every ingredient involved.

1½ cups chopped sunchokes (from about ¾ pound, peeled as best you can—doesn't need to be perfect)

1 heaping teaspoon kosher salt, plus more for the pot

1½ cups cooked or canned chickpeas (see Note, page 40), rinsed and drained

½ cup tahini paste

1 garlic clove (if garlic is too intense for you, feel free to use less)

Juice of ½ lemon

½ cup ice water

Toasted pine nuts, for serving

Hummus Vinaigrette (page 41) or 1 lemon plus extra-virgin olive oil, for serving

Aleppo pepper (za'atar or paprika will also work here), for serving

1   In a small pot, combine the sunchokes with water to cover and add a good pinch of salt. Bring to a boil over medium-high heat, cover, and cook until tender but not falling apart, about 10 minutes. Drain and let the sunchokes cool slightly.

2   In a blender or food processor, combine the cooked sunchokes, chickpeas, tahini, garlic, lemon juice, salt, and the ice water. Blend until smooth and creamy. (If making ahead, store the hummus in a jar in the fridge for up to 1 week.)

3   Put the hummus in a shallow bowl and sprinkle with toasted pine nuts (about 1 tablespoon per person) and the hummus vinaigrette (about 1 tablespoon per person), or the lazy version of a squeeze of lemon juice and a drizzle of olive oil. Finish with a pinch of Aleppo.

Zhug,
Red and Green

Zhug is a Yemeni hot sauce that features various combinations of chile peppers, spices, and in the case of the green version, fresh herbs. A dot or two of this stuff just brings your food to life.

RED ZHUG

Makes about ¾ cup

1 tablespoon coriander seeds, toasted in a
    dry pan until fragrant

2 teaspoons cumin seeds, toasted in a
    dry pan until fragrant

⅓ cup grapeseed oil

3 fresh hot red chile peppers, such as cayenne

1 garlic clove, peeled but left whole

1 teaspoon ground turmeric

1 teaspoon kosher salt

In a spice grinder, grind the toasted seeds until the mixture forms a powder. Transfer the mixture to a blender. Add the oil, chiles, garlic, turmeric, and salt and blend until it comes together. Store in a jar in the fridge for up to 1 month.

GREEN ZHUG

Makes about 1 cup

2 teaspoons coriander seeds, toasted in a
    dry pan until fragrant

2 teaspoons cumin seeds, toasted in a dry
    pan until fragrant

½ cup grapeseed oil

1 bunch flat-leaf parsley, thick stems removed

3 serrano peppers, stemmed

1 garlic clove, peeled but left whole

1 teaspoon ground turmeric

1 teaspoon kosher salt

In a spice grinder, grind the toasted seeds until the mixture forms a powder. Transfer the mixture to a blender. Add the oil, parsley, serranos, garlic, turmeric, and salt and blend until it comes together. Store in a jar in the fridge for up to 1 month.

NOTE *If you don't have a spice grinder, you can pound the toasted spices with mortar and pestle or blend them alone in the blender first.*

Labneh

Makes about 3 cups

When I discovered labneh—a thick, tangy yogurt that's like Greek yogurt's more interesting friend—it became a staple in my cooking. In Middle Eastern cuisine, you usually see it topped with za'atar and olive oil, but I use it slathered on sandwiches, dotted over grains, or smeared under roasted vegetables. Sometimes I go sweet and mix it with honey and fresh berries and top it with granola, or even bake it into cheesecake.

2 (32-ounce) containers whole-milk yogurt

2 tablespoons fresh lemon juice, plus more to taste

1 tablespoon kosher salt

In a large bowl, combine the yogurt, lemon juice, and salt and stir to combine. Line a large sieve with four layers of cheesecloth (large enough pieces so they generously drape over the side). Set the sieve in a smaller bowl so that it sits higher than the bottom of the bowl and pour the yogurt mixture into the sieve. Pull up the edges of the cloth around the yogurt. Place in the fridge and let the yogurt drain until it has thickened and a good amount of liquid has collected in the bowl, 12 to 24 hours (24 is ideal). If it's still not thick (it should be *thick*), let it go another 12 hours. Taste, and if it needs a bit more pop, add more lemon juice. Store the drained yogurt in a container in the fridge for up to 2 weeks.

Seven-Minute Eggs

Makes 6 eggs

I now have a serious soft-boiled egg habit, to the point that I'll buy an entire carton of eggs and cook them so I have them ready to go in the fridge at all times. In addition to being a quick and easy source of protein (essential for a mom who sometimes barely has time for a meal), these eggs make—I'm not kidding—every single dish better. They bring that extra-special little something that makes it seem like you put a lot of thought into a dish, when you and I both know you didn't. Their lusciously runny yolks enrich broths and soups, bring together bowls, act as a dressing on sandwiches and pitas, and bathe veggies (roasted, sautéed, grilled, raw) in their saucy, yolky glory.

How long you cook your eggs for is a personal preference—six minutes will get you a really runny yolk, while seven minutes is a little thicker and creamier.

6 large eggs, or however many you want to make

Fill a medium saucepan about three-quarters full with water and bring to a rapid boil. Carefully lower the eggs into the water and set a timer for 7 minutes. When the timer rings, immediately drain the eggs and run them under cold running water until completely cool. Peel the eggs and serve (or don't peel them and store in the refrigerator for up to 1 week).

Preserved Lemons

Makes 6 to 8 lemons (depending on their size)

Otherwise known as lemon pickle, this condiment is usually found in Indian and North African cooking and is every bit as briny, salty, and bright as it sounds. When I first learned about preserved lemons, it was such a lightbulb moment because I realized you can throw them into anything, and it takes it from good to showstopper. It's another one of those ingredients that people just can't put their finger on when trying to figure out what's making a dish so damn good. Luckily, they're super easy to make at home, which I do all the time so I always have a batch waiting for me on the counter.

8 lemons, scrubbed clean

½ cup kosher salt

1 to 1½ cups fresh lemon juice

1   Fill a large pot with water and bring to a boil. Carefully add a 1-quart mason jar so it's completely submerged. Remove the jar from the water and let it air-dry completely before making the lemons.

2   Use a sharp knife to score the bottom of the lemons so they're almost quartered but not cut all the way through into separate pieces. You could also thinly slice them, if you'd rather preserve them that way—up to you! Place the salt in a large bowl and add the lemons, rubbing them thoroughly with salt and making sure to get salt in all the nooks and crannies.

3   Stuff the lemons into the jar along with any salt remaining in the bowl, and fill the remaining space with the lemon juice. Cover and keep in a cool place for a minimum of 2 weeks but ideally 1 month. Store on your counter (though not in direct sunlight) or in your pantry—they'll keep pretty much forever.

Pickled, Herby, Charred Peppers

Makes about 4 cups

Growing up, there were always pickled peppers in our fridge. My dad loves them, and we'd take them out whenever we had a smoked meat brunch, or pretty much any other Sunday spread. I've made my own version of those peppers, and mine uses a simple pickling technique. Just make sure to char your peppers really well before pickling them so the pickles get fully infused with smoky flavor.

5 bell peppers (a mix of orange, yellow, and red)

⅔ cup extra-virgin olive oil

2 sprigs fresh oregano

¼ cup red wine vinegar

¼ cup balsamic vinegar

2 tablespoons torn fresh basil leaves

2 garlic cloves, thinly sliced

2 teaspoons kosher salt

2 teaspoons sugar

1 Using a gas stovetop burner or a grill and a pair of long tongs, char the peppers over an open flame until they're fully blackened and blistered all over. Place the charred peppers in a large bowl and cover with plastic wrap or a clean towel. Let the peppers steam for 20 minutes.

2 When the peppers are cool enough to handle, slip off the skins and pull out the cores and discard. Slice the peppers lengthwise and place them in a large jar with the olive oil, oregano, red wine vinegar, balsamic vinegar, basil, garlic, salt, and sugar. Shake the jar well to mix. Store in the fridge for at least 3 days before using, and up to 2 weeks. Let come to room temperature before serving so the oil can liquify again.

Pickled Beets, Radishes, and Onions

Makes 1 quart

There's something so gorgeous about a plate full of rosy-red jeweled pickles, which is exactly what you get when you throw a red beet in the mix and all of its juices bleed into the other vegetables. I also love the sweetness that you get from the beet, which brings out the natural sweetness of the onions and radishes, too—like vinegary candy.

2 small or 1 medium red beet

1 small red onion, thinly
   sliced into half-moons

10 radishes, halved,
   plus more as needed

2 garlic cloves, peeled
   but left whole

2 teaspoons mustard seeds

2 teaspoons coriander seeds

1 cup distilled white vinegar

⅓ cup sugar

2½ tablespoons kosher salt

1   Bring a large pot of water to a boil. Add an empty 1-quart jar and boil for 10 minutes. Carefully remove the jar and let air-dry.

2   Preheat the oven to 350°F.

3   Wrap the beet(s) together in foil and roast until a knife almost slides in, about 30 minutes. Remove the foil and carefully peel and slice the beet into ½-inch-thick pieces while it's hot. Layer the beet slices into the 1-quart jar, alternating with the onion and radishes.Depending on the size of your radishes, you may need more to fill your jar. Top with the garlic, mustard seeds, and coriander seeds.

4   In a medium saucepan, combine 1½ cups water, the vinegar, sugar, and salt. Bring the mixture to a boil over medium-high heat and cook, stirring, until the sugar and salt dissolve, about 5 minutes. Pour the hot brine over the vegetables so they are all completely submerged. Let the brine cool completely, then cover the jar and store in the fridge for at least 2 days to get nice and pickled, and up to 1 month.

Lemony Yogurt

Makes 1 cup

A bright, tangy, garlicky yogurt goes with pretty much anything and everything. And as you'll see in this book, I find an excuse to use it in a lot of my cooking. It's the perfect condiment for adding creaminess to a dish, to be the cool counterpart to hot chiles, and to bring out the other flavors on your plate. I love having this yogurt with almost all my egg dishes, on roasted meat and vegetables, and even dolloped on top of soups.

1 cup whole-milk Greek
   yogurt

Juice of ½ lemon

½ garlic clove, grated

½ teaspoon kosher salt,
   plus more to taste

In a medium bowl, whisk together the yogurt, lemon juice, garlic, and salt to combine. Check for seasoning and adjust if needed. Store in the fridge for up to 1 week.

Cauliflower-Turmeric Pickles

Makes 1 quart

I love turmeric, because of both its healing benefits and its happy, sunny color. When I open my fridge and see a jar of these vibrantly colored pickles, it just makes me feel like everything's going to be awesome.

1 cup distilled white vinegar

⅓ cup sugar

2½ tablespoons kosher salt

1½ teaspoons ground turmeric

1 small head of cauliflower, cut into small to medium florets

1 fresh spicy chile pepper of your choice, such as long hot or bird's-eye, halved lengthwise (optional)

3 garlic cloves, smashed

1 tablespoon coriander seeds

1 teaspoon black peppercorns

1   Bring a large pot of water to a boil. Add an empty 1-quart jar and boil for 10 minutes. Carefully remove the jar and let it air-dry.

2   In a large pot, combine the vinegar, sugar, salt, and turmeric with 1½ cups of water. Bring the mixture to a boil over medium-high heat and reduce the heat to medium-low. Let the mixture simmer for 5 minutes. Remove the pot from the heat.

3   Add the cauliflower, chile (if using), garlic, coriander seeds, and peppercorns to the 1-quart jar and pour over the liquid so the cauliflower is completely submerged. Let the brine cool completely, then cover the jar and store it in the fridge for at least 3 days before using, and up to 1 month (though the pickles will probably last longer).

Quick-Pickled Red Onion

Makes about 1 cup

I'm a huge fan of having pickles on the table, because they're the easiest way to add that necessary pop of acid that makes food taste so much better. But sometimes you don't have time to make a "proper" pickle, and that's when you reach for the quick pickle. It's a stupid-easy method you can also use for shallots and even chiles.

1 red onion, thinly sliced

⅔ cup red wine vinegar

1½ tablespoons sugar

1½ tablespoons kosher salt

In a medium jar, combine the onion, vinegar, sugar, salt, and ⅔ cup water. Close the lid and shake the jar very well, until the sugar and salt are dissolved. Let the pickles sit for at least 30 minutes before using. Store any leftovers in the fridge for up to 2 weeks.

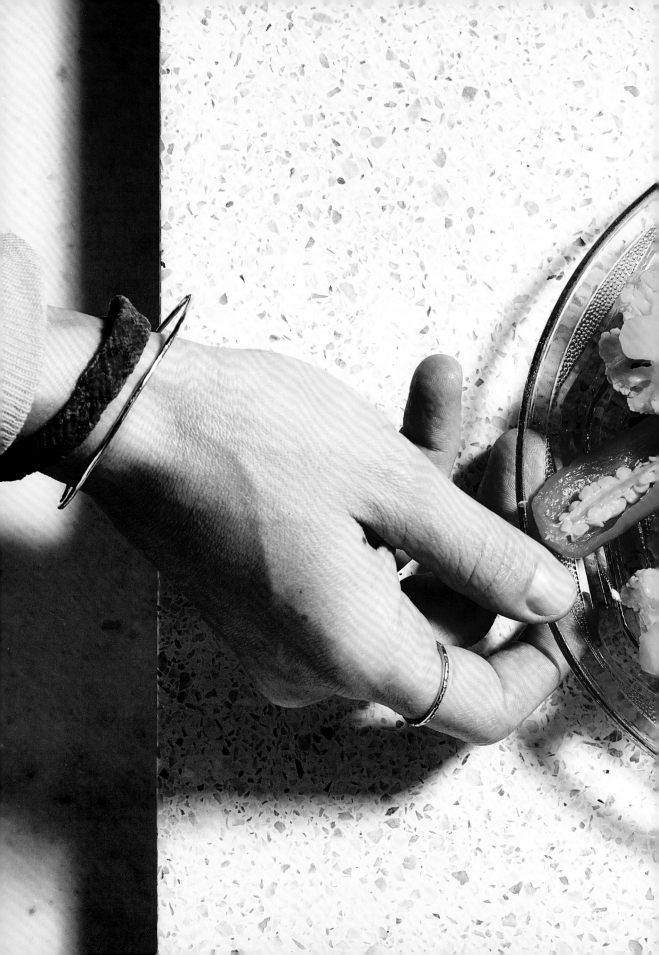

Cauliflower-Turmeric Pickles, page 57, and Pickled Beets, Radishes, and Onions, page 56

Dukkah

Makes about 1¼ cups

This Egyptian condiment is made up of toasted spices and nuts, which get ground together to create the ideal aromatic, textured finishing touch for pretty much any dish. It adds an extra-flavorful dimension to meat and vegetable dishes, and I really love it sprinkled over salads.

1 cup raw hazelnuts or
   shelled pistachios

1 teaspoon cumin seeds

1 teaspoon coriander seeds

3 tablespoons sesame seeds

½ teaspoon ground
   cardamom

1 teaspoon kosher salt

1 Preheat the oven to 350°F.

2 Spread the nuts on a baking sheet and toast until lightly golden, about 7 minutes. Let the nuts cool just enough to handle. Wrap the nuts in a clean towel and use the towel to slough off the skins. Set aside.

3 Heat a small dry skillet over medium-low heat. Add the cumin seeds and coriander seeds and toast briefly until fragrant and slightly golden, about 2 minutes. Set aside, separately from the nuts.

4 In the same pan, toast the sesame seeds until fragrant and slightly golden, 2 to 3 minutes.

5 In a blender, combine the cumin seeds, coriander seeds, and cardamom and blend briefly, until they just start to break down. Add the hazelnuts and blitz a few times more, making sure not to overblend. You want a chunky texture here, not nut butter.

6 Empty the mixture into a medium bowl and add the sesame seeds and salt. Store in an airtight container at room temperature for up to 2 months.

Eggs
All Day

Poached Eggs with Freekeh Tabbouleh, Yogurt, and Harissa

Serves 2

This is my riff on a traditional Turkish dish in which poached eggs are served with yogurt and finished with a chili-infused oil or butter. I love the original because of how the tanginess of the yogurt cuts right through the rich, runny yolks. But of course I had to put my own spin on it, so I serve the combination bowl-style over a celery-flecked freekeh tabbouleh with a generous drizzle of harissa oil. You could serve this over sourdough toast instead of the grains; it'll still be a lovely meal.

1 teaspoon kosher salt

2 tablespoons distilled white vinegar

4 large eggs

¼ cup Lemony Yogurt (page 56), Labneh (page 52), or plain yogurt with a large pinch of salt

2 tablespoons harissa, store-bought or homemade (see page 46), plus more as needed

Freekeh-Celery Tabbouleh (page 230), or 4 thick slices sourdough toast

Aleppo pepper or red chile flakes

Flaky sea salt

1   Fill a medium pot with about 5 inches of water and add the kosher salt. Bring the water to a boil over medium-high heat. Add the vinegar and create a gentle vortex in the water by swirling it in a circle with a spoon. Reduce the heat to low and carefully crack the eggs into the water one at a time. Continue gently stirring in a circular motion to keep the egg whites from getting too wispy. Cook for 3 minutes. Using a slotted spoon, transfer the eggs to a plate lined with paper towels to drain.

2   Schmear the bottom of two bowls with the lemony yogurt (about a couple tablespoons each), then top with 2 poached eggs. Drizzle with the harissa (I like using the oil that settles on top—use more than you think you need). Mound the tabbouleh next to the eggs, sprinkle everything with Aleppo and sea salt, and serve.

Classic Shakshuka with Garlicky Tahini

Serves 2 to 4

Shakshuka is basically eggs that are poached in a thick, spiced tomato-pepper sauce, sprinkled with herbs, and served in all of its runny, saucy sexiness with pita or challah. It's North African in origin, but you won't find a home in Israel that doesn't have this dish in steady rotation. Shakshuka is usually served for breakfast, but as you know, we Israelis are big fans of eggs all day, making this perfect for any meal, at any time. You can make a big batch of the sauce, keep it in the fridge, and then when you're ready to eat, all you have to do is ladle it into a pan and heat it up with some eggs. Make an individual portion if it's just for you, or definitely whip this out whenever you have to feed a whole bunch of people—just grab the biggest pan you have and cook 10 eggs at a time. Then all you need is a big loaf of fluffy white bread, challah, or a stack of pita, maybe a side salad, and you're solid.

One of the things I love most about shakshuka is that it's so fun to dress up with new flavors (like curry powder, which I've used here to add even more depth to the sauce). Sometimes I throw lamb meatballs in there, a sprinkle of feta, or chopped herbs like parsley or cilantro.

2 tablespoons extra-virgin olive oil, plus more for drizzling

1 small yellow onion, finely chopped

1 red bell pepper, finely chopped

Kosher salt and freshly ground black pepper

3 garlic cloves, finely chopped

1 teaspoon ground cumin

1 teaspoon curry powder (optional)

½ teaspoon ground turmeric

1 tablespoon harissa, store-bought or homemade (see page 46)

6 medium tomatoes, finely chopped, or 1 (28-ounce) can diced tomatoes (I like San Marzano)

Pinch of sugar

6 large eggs

Fresh dill or parsley, for garnish

Garlicky Tahini (page 37)

Challah, pita, or other soft white bread, for serving

1 In a large skillet with a fitted lid, heat 2 tablespoons olive oil over medium-high heat. Add the onion and bell pepper and season well with salt and black pepper. Cook until the onion just begins to lightly brown, 6 to 8 minutes, then add the garlic, cumin, curry powder (if using), turmeric, and harissa. Sauté until fragrant and the onion is lightly browned, 1 to 2 minutes. Stir in the tomatoes and season with the sugar and a pinch each of salt and black pepper. Cover the pan and simmer over low heat until the sauce has thickened slightly, about 20 minutes. Uncover the pan, raise the heat to medium-high, and continue simmering, stirring occasionally, until the sauce is thick enough to cling to the eggs, 10 to 15 minutes.

2 Use a large spoon to make 6 wells in the sauce. Crack an egg into each well, cover the pan with the lid, and cook over medium-high heat until the whites are set but the yolks are still runny, about 3 minutes.

3 Remove the pan from the heat. Garnish with fresh dill or parsley and drizzle with olive oil and garlicky tahini. Serve hot, with bread.

Masala Shakshuka with Cilantro-Mint Chutney

Serves 4 to 6

We're definitely more in Indian territory than Israeli here—a family of flavors I fell in love with when living there—but the idea is the same: Make a decadent, flavorful sauce for the eggs to lend their golden yolks to, top it off with a light, bright condiment (in this case, a fresh herb chutney instead of yogurt), and mop it all up with a stack of pita. This is more of a dinner shakshuka than lunch because the sauce takes time to thicken.

Cilantro-Mint Chutney

1 cup fresh cilantro leaves

½ cup fresh mint leaves

1 jalapeño, seeded

¼ cup plus 1 tablespoon grapeseed oil

Grated zest of 1 lime

Juice of ½ lime

1 teaspoon kosher salt

Shakshuka

6 medium tomatoes, or 1 (28-ounce) can crushed tomatoes

1 medium yellow onion, roughly chopped

½ cup fresh cilantro stems

1 jalapeño (if you want more spice, use a serrano, or whatever chile you'd like)

3 garlic cloves, peeled but left whole

2 tablespoons grapeseed oil

1 tablespoon mustard seeds

2 teaspoons garam masala

1 teaspoon cumin seeds

1 teaspoon ground turmeric

½ teaspoon ground coriander

2 (13.5-ounce) cans full-fat coconut milk

2 teaspoons kosher salt

6 large eggs

Fresh mint leaves, for serving

Pita, homemade (see page 150) or store-bought, for serving

1 Make the cilantro-mint chutney: In a blender or food processor, combine the cilantro, mint, jalapeño, oil, lime zest, lime juice, and salt and blend until smooth. Set aside.

2 Make the shakshuka: In a blender, combine the tomatoes, onion, cilantro stems, jalapeño, and garlic and blend until smooth. Set the tomato-onion mixture aside.

3 In a large skillet with a tightly fitted lid, heat the oil over medium heat. Add the mustard seeds. Once they start popping, add the garam masala, cumin seeds, turmeric, and coriander and toast until fragrant, about 30 seconds. Add the tomato-onion mixture and cook down, stirring occasionally, until it becomes paste-like, about 20 minutes.

4 Stir in the coconut milk and salt and cook for another 30 minutes to marry the flavors and thicken.

5 Use a large spoon to make 6 wells in the sauce. Crack an egg into each well, taking care not to break the yolks. Cover the pan and cook until the whites are just set and the yolks are still runny, about 3 minutes.

6 Serve with the chutney, fresh mint scattered on top, and pita.

PRO TIP *Use this sauce to poach fish or to serve with roasted vegetables or chicken.*

Classic Shakshuka with Garlicky Tahini, page 68

Very Green Shakshuka

Serves 2

This greened up version of shakshuka is such a fresh, fun twist on the classic. It gets super-hearty texture from greens like Swiss chard, parsley, and cilantro, plus a slightly sweet, anise-y flavor from the fennel. Finished off, obviously, with a drizzle of Green Tahini.

2 tablespoons extra-virgin olive oil

1 small yellow onion, finely diced

½ large or 1 small fennel bulb, trimmed, cored, and finely chopped (reserve the fronds for garnish, if available)

1 small jalapeño (seeded for less spice), finely chopped

1 garlic clove, finely chopped or grated

Kosher salt

1 teaspoon ground cumin

½ teaspoon ground coriander

4 large leaves Swiss chard or collards, midribs removed, leaves sliced into thin ribbons

2 tablespoons chopped fresh flat-leaf parsley

2 tablespoons chopped fresh cilantro, plus more for serving

¼ cup vegetable stock or water

4 large eggs

Freshly ground black pepper

Green Tahini (page 37), for serving

Fresh barbari or pita, homemade (see pages 146 and 150) or store-bought, for serving

1 Preheat the oven to 350°F.

2 In a large ovenproof skillet with a fitted lid, heat the oil over medium heat. Add the onion, fennel, jalapeño, garlic, and salt to taste and sauté until the vegetables are tender, 5 to 7 minutes. Add the cumin and coriander and sauté for another minute before adding the Swiss chard, parsley, and cilantro. Let the mixture sauté for another 2 to 3 minutes, then check for seasoning. Stir in the stock or water, cover, and cook until the greens are tender, 1 to 2 minutes.

3 Make 4 small wells in the mixture, crack the eggs into each of the dents, taking care not to break the yolks, and season with salt and pepper to taste. Transfer the pan, uncovered, to the oven and bake until the whites are just set and the yolks are still runny, 3 to 5 minutes.

4 Serve drizzled with the green tahini, topped with fennel fronds (if using) and cilantro, and with the flatbread.

Lamb Shakshuka with Lemony Yogurt

Serves 6

Lamb is one of my favorite meats to cook because of how rich and flavorful it is, so I figured it would be the perfect addition to a traditional shakshuka base. But then I wanted to see what would happen if I treated the whole situation like one big lamb kebab, using the same warm spices to make a gorgeous sauce for the eggs to poach in. I finished it with tart, lemon-laced yogurt for bright balance—long story short, major success.

2 teaspoons extra-virgin olive oil

1 small yellow onion, finely chopped

1½ teaspoons ground cumin

1 teaspoon sweet paprika

1 teaspoon ground turmeric

¼ teaspoon ground cinnamon

2 garlic cloves, minced

1 pound ground lamb

6 large tomatoes, chopped, or 1 (28-ounce) can crushed tomatoes

1 teaspoon kosher salt, plus more to taste

Freshly ground black pepper

6 large eggs

Fresh mint leaves, for serving

Lightly toasted pine nuts, for serving

Lemony Yogurt (page 56), for serving

Challah, pita, or other soft white bread, for serving

1 In a large skillet with a tight-fitting lid, heat the olive oil over medium-high heat. Add the onion and cook until soft, about 1 minute. Stir in the cumin, paprika, turmeric, and cinnamon and cook until fragrant, about 30 seconds. Add the garlic and lamb and cook until the meat browns and most of the liquid in the pan evaporates, 5 to 7 minutes. Use your spoon to break up any big chunks as the lamb cooks.

2 Stir in the tomatoes and sprinkle with the salt and a few cracks of black pepper. Cover the pan and reduce the heat to medium. Cook, stirring occasionally, until the tomatoes break down and form a beautiful caramelized sauce, 15 to 20 minutes. Remove the lid and cook for another 5 minutes to thicken slightly.

3 Create small wells in the sauce for the eggs to settle in. Crack an egg into each well, taking care not to break the yolks, and season with salt and pepper. Cover the pan and cook until the whites are set and the yolks are still runny, 3 to 5 minutes.

4 Serve with a sprinkle of mint and pine nuts, a drizzle of yogurt, and alongside your choice of bread.

Persian Mixed-Herb and Feta Frittata

Serves 6

Also known as *kuku sabzi*, this traditional Persian egg dish is loaded with fresh herbs, turning it a gorgeously bold green. I add my own twist with cream and feta, but it's still airy, light, and tastes as good as it makes you feel. Plus, it's great for entertaining because it's so easy to make that it's . . . kuku.

3 tablespoons extra-virgin olive oil

1 medium yellow onion, finely diced

1 garlic clove, grated or minced

1½ teaspoons kosher salt, plus more to taste

½ teaspoon ground cumin

½ teaspoon ground turmeric

½ teaspoon ground coriander

12 large eggs

¼ teaspoon freshly ground black pepper

1 cup chopped fresh parsley, plus more for serving

1 cup chopped fresh dill, plus more for serving

3 tablespoons finely chopped raw walnuts

½ cup heavy cream

1 cup crumbled sheep's milk feta

Lemony Yogurt (page 56), for serving

Hot sauce of your choice (I love Red Zhug, page 50, with this), for serving

1 Preheat the oven to 350°F.

2 In a large cast-iron skillet, heat 1 tablespoon of the olive oil over medium heat. Add the onion and cook until it begins to soften, about 3 minutes. Add the garlic, salt, cumin, turmeric, and coriander and continue cooking for 1 minute. Set aside.

3 In a large bowl, whisk the eggs until uniform. Season with a pinch of salt and the black pepper, then add the onion mixture, parsley, dill, walnuts, and cream. Mix thoroughly and set aside.

4 In the same skillet, heat the remaining 2 tablespoons olive oil over medium heat. Carefully rotate the pan so the olive oil coats the entire bottom plus a few inches up the sides. Add the egg mixture and cook undisturbed until the sides begin to set, 3 to 5 minutes.

5 Sprinkle the eggs with the feta and transfer the pan to the oven. Bake until the eggs are almost set but still a little jiggly on top, 15 to 20 minutes.

6 Serve topped with extra parsley and dill and alongside lemony yogurt and hot sauce.

Israeli Breakfast Bowl

Serves 2

Israelis just win when it comes to breakfast; they know how to do it right. There's always eggs (obvi), tahini and other schmears for dipping, and fresh white cheese—I used sheep's milk feta in this case—plus the signature Israeli chopped salad with tomatoes, cucumbers, and red onion. It's a lot going on, but just enough to make you feel satisfied and energized, not like you need a nap. I'm never gonna knock bacon and pancakes, but let's be honest, that's not exactly starting your day with a bang. To me, this is such a beautiful example of the Mediterranean way—living life in moderation and building vegetables into every meal. For this version, I call for frying the eggs with a sprinkle of Aleppo (so the red oily goodness seeps into the eggs and you get that hit of spice), but you could prepare the eggs any way you like. And if you don't want to commit to the entire chopped salad recipe, just halve the amount of vegetables and you're good to go.

4 tablespoons extra-virgin olive oil

2 tablespoons za'atar, store-bought or homemade (see page 31)

4 large eggs

2 teaspoons Aleppo pepper or red chile flakes

Kosher salt and freshly ground black pepper

1 cup Classic Hummus (page 40) or Garlicky Tahini (page 37)

1 cup labneh, store-bought or homemade (see page 52)

Chopped Salad (page 114)

4 ounces feta, crumbled (I love Bulgarian)

Chopped fresh parsley and dill, for garnish

Easy Peasy Pita (page 150), Nan-e Barbari (page 146), All the Seeds Challah (page 151), or store-bought breads, for serving

Hot sauce, for serving

1   In a small bowl, combine 3 tablespoons of the olive oil with the za'atar. Set aside.

2   In a medium skillet, heat 1 tablespoon of the olive oil over medium-high heat for about 2 minutes to make sure it's nice and hot. When the oil shimmers, crack the eggs into the oil and sprinkle with the Aleppo. Season with a pinch of salt and black pepper as the eggs fry. Cook until the whites are set but the yolks are still runny, 2 to 3 minutes.

3   In the bottom of each of two bowls, scoop the hummus or tahini on one side and the labneh on the other side. Using a clean spoon for each, make a quick swoosh in the middle of the dollops to create a well. Fill the well with a drizzle of the za'atar olive oil. Place the salad and the feta around the dips and finish with the eggs to the side, so you can see all the beautiful ingredients. Garnish with fresh herbs and serve with bread and hot sauce of your choice.

Baked at Brunch

Most of the time in our house, the first meal of the day is something grabbed out of the fridge,

slathered with tahini and homemade hot sauce, and inhaled while standing over the counter before running out the door for work. That's why I'm a big fan of keeping partially prepped dishes on hand—roasted veg, cooked grains, soft-boiled eggs, relishes, condiments, pickles, fresh pita—so I can just toss something together for a quick bite. If people are coming over for brunch, though, that's a different story—but not by much. I'm always a fan of making food that's easy to assemble and to scale for 3 or 6 or 10. That's why when I'm feeding a group in the morning, there's usually a savory option like shakshuka (see pages 68–74) or a frittata (see page 77) in the mix, or some kind of flatbread or pita situation. But I also like to make at least one dish that's a little above and beyond and fresh out of the oven (or baked the night before), which is where these recipes come in. These are the crowd-pleasers, the showstoppers. I guarantee if you pull out a fresh loaf of Date Banana Bread with Coconut Crumble (page 85), a pan of Salted Tahini-Chocolate Babka Buns (page 87), or a pretty container filled with granola that you made from scratch (see page 91), your guests are going to lose their minds—in the best possible way. These recipes do take a little extra effort, but they go a long way to making people feel special.

Date Banana Bread with Coconut Crumble

Makes 1 loaf

There are many, many variations of banana bread out there, and I've tried and loved almost every single one of them. So it felt absolutely necessary to include one with the addition of some of my favorite flavors, including Medjool dates, which I fell in love with when I was living in Israel. This version isn't overly sweet, namely because it uses plump dates instead of a ton of sugar. Their honey-caramel, jammy, candy flavor brings out the natural sweetness of the banana and coconut. Since I'll take any opportunity I can get to add a crumb topping, this bread also gets a coconut-walnut crumble that takes the cake to the next level. I love slathering this bread with room-temp butter, creamy date jam, and honey, and finishing with a sprinkle of sea salt. I'm drooling just thinking about it.

Coconut-Walnut Crumb Topping

¼ cup roughly chopped raw walnuts

⅓ cup all-purpose flour

¼ cup unsweetened coconut flakes

3 tablespoons unsalted butter, at room temperature or melted

½ teaspoon ground cinnamon

½ teaspoon kosher salt

Banana Bread

8 tablespoons (1 stick) unsalted butter, melted and cooled slightly, plus more for the pan

1½ cups all-purpose flour, plus more for the pan

1 cup packed dark brown sugar

3 ripe bananas, mashed

1 **Make the coconut-walnut crumb topping:** In a medium bowl, combine the walnuts, flour, coconut flakes, brown sugar, butter, cinnamon, and kosher salt. Mix until a crumble texture has formed. Set aside.

2 **Make the banana bread:** Preheat the oven to 350°F. Butter and flour an 8½ x 4½-inch loaf pan.

3 In a large bowl, use a hand mixer or whisk to combine the melted butter with the brown sugar, bananas, dates, yogurt or sour cream, eggs, and vanilla. Try to break up the dates and bananas as well as you can.

4 In another large bowl, whisk together the flour, shredded coconut, baking soda, cinnamon, and kosher salt.

5 Add half of the flour mixture to the banana mixture and mix until just combined. Repeat with the remaining flour mixture. Fold in the walnuts (if using) and pour the batter into the prepared loaf pan.

6 Sprinkle the crumb topping over the batter, then gently press the batter with your fingers so some of the topping gets pushed inside the bread.

(recipe and ingredients continue)

6 Medjool dates, pitted and roughly chopped (about ½ cup)

⅓ cup whole-milk yogurt or sour cream

2 large eggs

1 teaspoon vanilla extract

½ cup unsweetened shredded coconut

1½ teaspoons baking soda

1 teaspoon ground cinnamon

1 teaspoon kosher salt

⅓ cup lightly toasted and chopped walnuts (optional)

Serving

Salted butter

Flaky sea salt

Honey

Date Jam (right)

7   Place the pan on a baking sheet (to catch any drips) and bake until a skewer or cake tester comes out clean, 1 hour to 1 hour 15 minutes. If the bread starts to get too dark, tent it with foil. Let cool slightly.

8   **To serve:** Slice the banana bread and top with butter, a sprinkle of sea salt, a drizzle of honey, and jam.

DATE JAM

Makes about 1 cup

Dates were basically born to be made into a sticky, just-the-right-amount-of-sweet jam that goes well with anything you're serving in the morning.

20 Medjool dates, pitted

In a small pot, combine the dates with 2 cups of water. Over medium heat, simmer the dates as you break them up with a spoon. Once they start breaking down, after 3 to 5 minutes, transfer the mixture to a blender and blend until creamy. Transfer the mixture back to the pot and cook over medium heat until it thickens to a jamlike consistency, 5 to 10 minutes. Remove the pot from the heat and allow the jam to cool before storing it in a jar in the fridge for up to 1 week.

Salted Tahini-Chocolate Babka Buns

Makes 12 buns

For anyone who isn't already obsessed, babka is a traditional Jewish dessert that's a buttery yeasted loaf swirled with gooey chocolate or cinnamon layers. I made it my mission to come up with a version that was (a) home cook friendly and (b) a mash-up with the brunch-must-have, cinnamon buns. I worked some citrus zest into the dough itself, which lightens the flavor, and the drizzle of tahini over the chocolate filling keeps things from getting crazy sweet, but don't worry . . . I added a salted sugar glaze to give it that extra somethin' somethin'. I mean . . . come on! Ayv freaked over these.

Dough

1¼ cups whole milk

1 envelope (2¼ teaspoons) active dry yeast

5¼ cups loosely packed all-purpose flour, plus more for kneading and rolling out

½ cup sugar

1½ teaspoons kosher salt

4 large eggs

1 teaspoon vanilla extract

Grated zest of 1 orange

Grated zest of 1 lemon

8 tablespoons (1 stick) unsalted butter, at room temperature, plus more for greasing the bowl

Tahini-Chocolate Filling

2 cups finely chopped bittersweet chocolate

4 tablespoons (½ stick) unsalted butter

½ cup tahini paste

½ teaspoon kosher salt

¼ teaspoon ground cinnamon

1   Make the dough: In a small saucepan, warm the milk over medium heat until it's almost hot, or just about body temperature, 1 to 2 minutes. (Take care not to get the milk too hot or it will kill the yeast!) In a small bowl, stir together the milk and yeast and let it sit for at least 10 minutes, until foamy.

2   In a stand mixer fitted with the dough hook, combine the flour, sugar, and salt. Mix briefly on low speed to combine. Add the milk-yeast mixture, eggs, vanilla, orange zest, and lemon zest and mix until combined. You may want to occasionally stop the mixer and use a spatula to scrape down the sides and bottom of the bowl to make sure all of the ingredients are mixed in. Continue mixing until the dough has come together and is smooth.

3   With the mixer running, begin adding the butter 1 tablespoon at a time, waiting to add more until the last tablespoon is fully incorporated. Mix on medium speed until the dough is still a bit sticky but holds together, 10 to 15 minutes.

4   Turn the dough out onto a floured work surface. Sprinkle the top of the dough with more flour and knead until it is smooth and not quite as tacky as it was before, 3 to 5 minutes. Place the dough in a large bowl greased with butter and cover with plastic wrap. You can proof the dough one of two ways: in the fridge overnight (which makes it so much easier to roll out and fill; it will double in size) or in a warm place for 1 hour 30 minutes or until it doubles in size.

(recipe and ingredients continue)

Salted Sugar Glaze

¾ cup heavy cream

8 tablespoons (1 stick) unsalted butter

½ cup packed dark brown sugar

¾ teaspoon kosher salt

5 Make the tahini-chocolate filling: In a medium pot, bring 1 to 2 inches of water to a simmer over medium-high heat. Set a heatproof bowl over the pot (make sure it's not touching the water) and add 1½ cups of the chocolate and the butter. Allow the chocolate and butter to melt completely, stirring occasionally, about 6 minutes. Remove the bowl from the heat and fold in the tahini, salt, and cinnamon. Place the filling in the fridge to cool for 20 minutes.

6 Preheat the oven to 350°F. Line a large baking sheet with parchment paper and set aside.

7 Turn the dough out onto a clean floured work surface. You have to work quickly here: Roll it out into a rectangle that's about ¼ inch thick. Spread the cooled melted chocolate mixture all over the dough, covering the surface as evenly as possible. Then sprinkle the remaining ½ cup chopped chocolate over the top. Starting from a long side, roll the dough tightly. Slice the roll crosswise into 12 equal pieces and arrange them on the prepared baking sheet cut-sides up. Cover the buns with a damp towel and proof in a warm environment for 20 minutes. (Near your warming oven is great—but not on top of it!)

8 Bake the buns: Uncover the buns and bake until the dough is firm and set on the outside, 20 to 30 minutes.

9 Make the salted sugar glaze: In a small pot, combine the cream, butter, brown sugar, and salt. Set over medium heat and whisk the mixture occasionally as it melts. The moment it reaches a simmer, remove the pot from the heat. Immediately drizzle half over the warm buns, which will ensure that it soaks in. Serve the rest of the glaze on the side for dipping.

VARIATION

Simple Syrup Glaze

I love how the salted sugar glaze in the standard recipe is a little extra, but if you want to take the richness down a notch, make this simple syrup version instead.

In a small saucepan, combine ½ cup sugar with ½ cup water. Bring to a simmer over medium heat and cook until the sugar dissolves, about 5 minutes. Brush over the warm-out-of-the-oven buns.

Epic Seedy Granola

Makes about 4 cups

You know how in *Clueless* Cher attempts to bake cookies to give her house a warm, cozy smell? She really should have been making granola, which is straight-up the easiest way to make your home smell ah-mazing. And the best part is then you have your very own from-scratch granola, which is always going to be more impressive and delicious than store-bought. For my version, I wanted to highlight a whole mess of seeds—sunflower, pumpkin, sesame, poppy—and a hint of maple syrup. And as hard as I tried not to call for tahini here—which is pretty much a joke at this point—I couldn't resist adding that rich, deep flavor to round it all out. The final product reminds me of a honey-caramelized sesame seed candy I grew up eating in Israel. Divine.

1 cup unsweetened coconut flakes

½ cup sunflower seeds

½ cup pumpkin seeds

½ cup sesame seeds

¼ cup poppy seeds

¼ cup flaxseeds

½ cup maple syrup

2 tablespoons unrefined coconut oil, melted

2 tablespoons tahini paste

1 teaspoon kosher salt

½ teaspoon vanilla extract

½ cup dried fruit (optional), such as cherries, apricots (roughly chopped), currants, or raisins

1 Preheat the oven to 350°F. Line a sheet pan with parchment paper or a silicone baking mat.

2 In a large bowl, combine the coconut flakes, all the seeds, maple syrup, coconut oil, tahini, salt, and vanilla. Mix thoroughly with a spatula to make sure the mixture is well coated and spread the mixture evenly on the prepared sheet pan. Bake until the mixture is a deep golden brown and smells nice and toasty, about 35 minutes, making sure to toss and mix it every 10 minutes or so to prevent burning. If you're using a silicone mat that's slightly smaller than your sheet pan, try to keep everything on the mat or it will stick to the pan and you won't be able to get it off without soaking it in water. That means less granola for you to eat, which will make you sad.

3 Remove the pan from the oven and allow the granola to cool before tossing it with the dried fruit (if using) and storing in an airtight container at room temperature for up to 2 weeks.

NOTE

Orange Blossom Yogurt: *For a no-frills-but-magical morning offering, I love serving the granola over honey-sweetened yogurt with orange blossom water, which has an amazing floral, perfume-y quality. To serve two, in a medium bowl, whisk together 2 cups whole-milk Greek yogurt and 1 tablespoon honey. Fold in 2 teaspoons orange blossom water. Divide the yogurt between two bowls and top with ¼-inch-thick orange slices (peel and pith removed), some of the granola, a sprinkle of cinnamon, and a drizzle of honey.*

Pistachio-Cardamom Coffee Cake

Serves 12

When I started experimenting with a Middle Eastern take on coffee cake, my initial thought was to add cardamom—one of my favorite warm, comforting spices. At first I was playing it safe and the cake was . . . nice. Cute but not a lot of personality. But then I really went for it, cranked up the cardamom notes, added bright, floral lemon zest, and folded in ground pistachios for their vibrant green color and subtly sweet, nutty flavor, and things got much, much sexier.

Streusel

1 cup all-purpose flour

½ cup raw pistachios, roughly chopped

½ cup packed dark brown sugar

8 tablespoons (1 stick) unsalted butter, melted

¼ cup granulated sugar

½ teaspoon ground cardamom

½ teaspoon kosher salt

¼ teaspoon ground cinnamon

Coffee Cake

1½ sticks (6 ounces) unsalted butter, at room temperature, plus more for the baking dish

1¾ cups all-purpose flour

¾ cup raw pistachios, finely ground in a food processor

2 teaspoons ground cardamom

1½ teaspoons baking powder

1 teaspoon kosher salt

½ teaspoon baking soda

½ teaspoon ground cinnamon

¾ cup granulated sugar

¼ cup packed dark brown sugar

3 large eggs, at room temperature

Grated zest of 1 lemon

1 teaspoon vanilla extract

1¼ cups whole-milk yogurt or sour cream, at room temperature

¼ cup whole milk, at room temperature

1 **Make the streusel:** In a medium bowl, combine the flour, chopped pistachios, brown sugar, melted butter, granulated sugar, cardamom, salt, and cinnamon. Using a spatula, wooden spoon, or just your hands, mix until thoroughly combined and crumbly. Set aside.

2 **Make the coffee cake:** Preheat the oven to 350°F. Grease an 8 × 8-inch baking dish with butter and line it with a piece of parchment, really smoothing it all to the edge and in the corners as much as possible.

3 In a medium bowl, whisk together the flour, ground pistachios, cardamom, baking powder, salt, baking soda, and cinnamon. Set aside.

4 In a stand mixer fitted with the paddle attachment (or in a large bowl with a handheld mixer or spoon), cream the butter, granulated sugar, and brown sugar on medium speed until very light and airy, about 5 minutes. Stop the mixer periodically to scrape down the bowl with a spatula to make sure no ingredients get left behind. Add the eggs one at a time, mixing until each egg is incorporated before adding the next. Add the lemon zest and vanilla and mix until combined. Add the yogurt and milk and continue mixing until the batter is uniform.

5 Gently fold in the flour mixture in two stages with a spatula until just combined, then give it one good whip at the end so everything is evenly incorporated.

6 Pour half of the batter into the prepared baking dish and spread it out on the bottom evenly. Scatter one-third of the streusel on top. Evenly pour over the rest of the batter and scatter the rest of the streusel on top.

7 Bake until a skewer or cake tester comes out clean, 45 to 55 minutes. If the cake looks like it's getting too dark as it bakes or the pistachios start to lose their green color, place a piece of foil on top. Let cool in the baking dish and serve.

Salads
and
Fresh
Bites

There are no rules for when or how you serve these dishes;

they're just the perfect recipes to reach for when you want something light and fresh. Choose one or two to serve before the main event or combine a few to make a meal. They're especially great for when people end up sticking around for lunch or dinner and you need something quick and easy to throw together, or when you're walking in the door after work and need something to eat ASAP. In many cases, it's just a matter of assembling staples and essentials that you'll likely already have on hand, then tossing in a bunch of fresh veg, herbs, seeds, or nuts.

Slow-Roasted and Fresh Cherry Tomato Salad with Feta, Basil, and Honey

Serves 4

I'm a tomato freak, so in the summer they're basically all I want to eat. I came up with this salad as a way to get my fix and to showcase tomatoes in both their raw and roasted forms. The roasted tomatoes contrast with the fresh ones with their concentrated sweetness. Everything gets tossed with a roasted garlic vinaigrette and topped with onions for their spicy crunch, creamy sheep's milk feta, and tons of fresh basil. Serve this one with plenty of crusty bread to sop up all the delicious juices that mingle at the bottom of the bowl.

Roasted Tomatoes

3 cups cherry tomatoes

1 head of garlic, separated into cloves (about 12), but unpeeled

2 tablespoons extra-virgin olive oil

1 tablespoon honey

2 teaspoons Urfa pepper, cayenne pepper, or chili powder

Kosher salt and freshly ground black pepper

Dressing

1 tablespoon plus 1 teaspoon red wine vinegar

1 teaspoon honey

½ teaspoon kosher salt, plus more to taste

¼ teaspoon freshly ground black pepper, plus more to taste

3 tablespoons extra-virgin olive oil

Serving

3 cups cherry tomatoes, halved

½ small red onion, finely chopped

⅓ cup feta

Handful of fresh basil leaves

Urfa pepper or red chile flakes

Flaky sea salt

Sourdough bread

1 **Roast the tomatoes:** Preheat the oven to 300°F.

2 In a baking dish, combine the cherry tomatoes, garlic, olive oil, honey, and Urfa pepper. Sprinkle with kosher salt and black pepper to taste and use your hands to give everything a good toss. Roast until the tomatoes are blistered, soft, and caramelized, 1 hour. When they are cool enough to handle, peel the garlic cloves.

3 **Make the dressing:** In a medium bowl, combine the vinegar, honey, kosher salt, and black pepper. Add 6 of the roasted garlic cloves and whisk to combine. While whisking, slowly stream in the olive oil and continue whisking until the dressing is smooth and emulsified. Adjust the seasoning with more kosher salt and black pepper to taste, if desired.

4 **To serve:** Scatter the halved fresh tomatoes and the red onion in a shallow bowl. Add the roasted tomatoes and remaining garlic cloves and give everything a toss. Crumble the feta over the top and finish with the dressing, basil, and a sprinkle of Urfa and flaky sea salt to taste. Serve with plenty of crusty bread.

Herby Seeds Salad with Toasted Cumin Vinaigrette

Serves 2 to 4

I actually think I have an herb problem. To me, a dish doesn't feel complete unless I make it rain fresh, green leaves. Or in this case, use just about as much dill and parsley as I do lettuce. When dressed properly and partnered with the right ingredients, fresh herbs elevate a salad, giving it a garden-fresh flavor and aroma that you just want to dive into. The toasted cumin vinaigrette grounds the dish with an earthiness that always has people guessing what the secret ingredient is, but the herbs are still the star of the show.

1 **Make the dressing:** In a medium bowl, whisk together the shallot, lemon zest, vinegar, lemon juice, honey, and cumin seeds. Continue whisking as you slowly drizzle in the olive oil. Whisk in the salt and pepper. Set aside.

2 **Assemble the salad:** On a large platter, lay down the lettuce leaves and layer the avocados and radish over the top. Sprinkle with the toasted pumpkin, sunflower, and sesame seeds and drizzle with the dressing. Finish with the dill, parsley, and mint and serve.

Dressing

1 shallot, finely chopped

Grated zest of 1 lemon

1 tablespoon plus 1 teaspoon red wine vinegar

1 tablespoon fresh lemon juice

1 tablespoon honey

1 teaspoon cumin seeds, toasted in a dry pan until fragrant

¼ cup extra-virgin olive oil

1 teaspoon kosher salt

½ teaspoon freshly ground black pepper

Salad

2 heads Little Gem lettuce, leaves separated

2 avocados, sliced

1 radish, thinly sliced (watermelon, breakfast, purple—any will do)

2 tablespoons pumpkin seeds, toasted in a dry pan until fragrant

2 tablespoons sunflower seeds, toasted in a dry pan until fragrant

2 teaspoons sesame seeds, toasted in a dry pan until fragrant

¼ cup chopped fresh dill

¼ cup chopped fresh parsley

¼ cup chopped fresh mint

Spicy Fried Eggplant Salad with Dill

Serves 4 to 6

Okay, we're taking some liberties in calling this a salad because it's essentially a big pile of garlicky fried eggplant dressed with a vinaigrette. And I've literally never seen a vegetable soak up more oil in my life—you're going to use more oil here than you're maybe comfortable with and just need to erase it from your memory and never look back. But I'm not mad about it, because the result is a hearty, oily-in-all-the-right-ways dish that still manages to taste bright and fresh thanks to the vinegar. It's a dish that's inspired by the pickled eggplant (which I'm completely addicted to) that my mother-in-law always has in her impressively stocked fridge. Definitely make this one ahead and let the eggplant soak up all the vinaigrette; it gets better as it sits.

Eggplant

4 small eggplants, sliced into ¼-inch-thick rounds

1 teaspoon kosher salt, plus more to taste

1 cup grapeseed oil, plus more if needed

Dressing

⅔ cup extra-virgin olive oil

⅓ cup plus 2 tablespoons red wine vinegar

¼ cup chopped fresh dill

1 tablespoon honey

1 tablespoon Aleppo pepper or red chile flakes

2 teaspoons kosher salt

Assembly

1 shallot, thinly sliced

1 garlic clove, thinly sliced

1 tablespoon Aleppo pepper or red chile flakes

Fresh dill, for garnish

NOTE *I also love piling up the eggplant on labneh-schmeared sourdough toast (see page 52).*

1 Cook the eggplant: Arrange the eggplant slices in a single layer on a baking sheet and sprinkle with the salt. Let the eggplant sit at room temperature for 20 to 30 minutes while the salt draws out the extra water from the eggplant. Pat the slices dry with a paper towel and sprinkle with more salt.

2 In a large skillet, heat ½ cup of the grapeseed oil over medium-high heat until it shimmers (grapeseed oil has a higher smoke point than olive oil, which makes it great for frying). Working in batches so you don't crowd the pan, fry the eggplant until it's nice and crisp on both sides, 3 to 4 minutes per side. Don't be afraid to add more oil to the pan as needed—eggplant tends to soak it up like a sponge. Transfer the eggplant to a plate or sheet pan lined with paper towels to drain.

3 Make the dressing: In a medium bowl, whisk together the olive oil, vinegar, dill, honey, Aleppo pepper, and salt. Set aside.

4 Assemble the salad: Arrange the fried eggplant on a large platter and layer on the sliced shallot, garlic, and Aleppo. Drizzle with the dressing, sprinkle with dill, and serve.

Shaved Fennel, Celery, and Mint Salad

Serves 4

Coming up with a concept for a simple salad is hard for me, because my instinct is to load and load and load until you have this crazy mess of ingredients. Not cute. You have to show restraint—of which I have zero—but when I saw how clean and fresh the fennel, celery, and mint are on their own, I didn't want to mess much with it. All I did was add grated pecorino for its natural saltiness, plus toasted pine nuts for texture, and I ended up with a salad where every time I make it—I kid you not—*everyone* asks for the recipe. It's also the easiest thing to make. If you have a mandoline, you can rock this salad anywhere you go.

2 fennel bulbs, trimmed (fronds reserved), bulb halved horizontally

3 celery stalks

1 cup pine nuts, toasted and roughly chopped (you can also blitz briefly in a blender or food processor)

1 cup finely grated pecorino or Parmesan (I love a Microplane for this)

¼ cup plus 2 tablespoons extra-virgin olive oil

Grated zest and juice of 1 lemon

1½ teaspoons kosher salt

¼ cup fresh mint leaves, torn (or keep whole if the leaves are small)

1   Roughly tear about 2 tablespoons of the fennel fronds. I recommend using the bits of the frond that are closest to the bulb; they're more tender. Set aside.

2   Over a large bowl, use a mandoline to thinly slice the fennel horizontally (about ¼ inch thick; any thinner and it will get too wilty). Repeat with the celery. Add the pine nuts and pecorino and toss gently to combine. Pour over the olive oil, add the lemon zest, lemon juice, and salt and toss again to coat. Sprinkle with the torn fennel fronds and mint and serve.

Summer Pita Fattoush with Peaches, Tomatoes, and Basil

Serves 6

This is a cousin of panzanella—or Italian bread salad—but instead of dried bread, you use toasted pita. For this version, we're full-on summer with the combination of peaches and tomatoes, which are both poppin' at the market around the same time and make a natural pair with their sweet-sourness. (Remember to use only the ripest, juiciest, in-season peaches and tomatoes you can find!) All that's left to do is whisk together a light dressing, throw in a couple handfuls of fresh herbs, and give it a good dusting of bright, citrusy sumac.

Toasted Pita

2 pitas, homemade (see page 150) or store-bought, torn into bite-size pieces

¼ cup extra-virgin olive oil

Kosher salt

Dressing

Juice of ½ lemon

1½ teaspoons honey

1 teaspoon red wine vinegar

3 tablespoons extra-virgin olive oil

Kosher salt and freshly ground black pepper

Salad

2 cups roughly chopped tomatoes (I like to get all different types and colors)

1 peach, thinly sliced

Handful of fresh basil leaves, torn

Handful of fresh mint leaves, torn

Handful of fresh parsley leaves, torn

1 small red onion, thinly sliced

Sumac

1 **Toast the pita:** Preheat the oven to 350°F.

2 In a medium bowl, combine the torn pita pieces with the olive oil and a large pinch of salt. Toss to coat. Spread the pita on a sheet pan and toast in the oven until crisp and golden, about 8 minutes (start checking after 5). Set aside to cool.

3 **Make the dressing:** In a medium bowl, whisk together the lemon juice, honey, and vinegar. Continue whisking as you slowly drizzle in the olive oil. Season with salt and pepper to taste.

4 **Assemble the salad:** In a large bowl, combine the tomatoes, peach, basil, mint, parsley, onion, and the toasted pita. Toss with the dressing and finish with a sprinkle of sumac.

Vinegar and Honey–Roasted Beets with Labneh

Serves 4

I love roasting beets with vinegar and honey and letting the oven do its thing. The acidity from the vinegar balances out the beets' dense earthiness while the honey brings out their natural sweetness and almost candies them. Spooned over rich, tangy labneh—roasting juices and all. You could just stop there and have a really solid dish, but I also like to add a gremolata made with the beet greens. They're not only gorgeous when their color bleeds out over the yogurt, but they also have a deep Swiss chard–like flavor. I recommend serving this with plenty of fresh pita or Nan-e Barbari (page 146), especially the nigella and olive oil version. And definitely throw a few extra beets into the oven so you can make French Lentils with Beets, Sour Cherries, Urfa, and Almonds (page 118) the next day for lunch.

Roasted Beets

6 small beets, a mix of yellow and red, with leafy tops removed and stems reserved, well scrubbed

3 tablespoons red wine vinegar

3 tablespoons honey

3 strips of orange zest

1 teaspoon coriander seeds

1 teaspoon kosher salt

Beet Stem Gremolata

¼ cup finely chopped reserved beet stems

¼ cup chopped fresh parsley

1 small garlic clove, grated

Grated zest of 1 small or ½ large orange

3 tablespoons extra-virgin olive oil

1 tablespoon red wine vinegar

2 teaspoons honey

½ teaspoon kosher salt

Serving

1 cup labneh, store-bought or homemade (see page 52)

Sumac

Easy Peasy Pita (page 150) or Nan-e Barbari (page 146)

1 **Roast the beets:** Preheat the oven to 350°F.

2 In a large bowl, combine the beets, vinegar, honey, orange zest, coriander seeds, salt, and 1 tablespoon water. Toss to coat. Arrange the beets on a rimmed baking sheet and cover the tray tightly with foil. Roast until the beets can be easily pierced with a knife, about 45 minutes. I like to wait until almost all the liquid has evaporated and you get to roll the beets around in the sticky juice that forms on the bottom. Roast for another 5 minutes until the skin caramelizes and forms an almost candied shell. Once the beets are cool enough to handle, cut them into 1-inch-thick wedges.

3 **Make the beet stem gremolata:** In a medium bowl, combine the beet stems, parsley, garlic, and orange zest. Mix gently to combine. Dress the mixture with the olive oil, vinegar, and honey, season with the salt, and toss until evenly coated.

4 **To serve:** In a large bowl, combine the beets and gremolata and toss to coat. Spread the labneh on a platter and place the dressed beets on top, including any juices that have accumulated in the bowl. Add a sprinkle of sumac and serve with flatbread.

Raw Carrot Salad with Dates, Walnuts, and Aleppo

Serves 6

The beauty of this simple salad—besides the fact it takes raw carrots to a *whole* new place—is that the dressing marinates and tenderizes the carrots. So while you're sitting around the table chitchatting and picking at things, this will get better and better as the carrots wilt. That's also great news if you're not able to slice the carrots into a thin julienne—no need to get precious about it! And definitely use any leftovers as a slaw on sandwiches.

¼ cup extra-virgin olive oil

Grated zest and juice of 1 lemon

1 tablespoon honey

1 small garlic clove, grated

1 teaspoon kosher salt

½ teaspoon Aleppo pepper or red chile flakes, plus more (optional) for serving

¼ teaspoon freshly ground black pepper

2 bunches of medium carrots (around 12 carrots total), sliced lengthwise and cut into thin matchsticks

1 small red onion, very thinly sliced (a mandoline is perfect here)

4 Medjool dates, pitted and chopped

½ cup raw walnuts, roughly chopped or quickly blitzed (I like a mix of large and small chunks)

1 In a medium bowl, combine the olive oil, lemon zest, lemon juice, honey, garlic, salt, Aleppo pepper, and black pepper. Whisk until emulsified and set aside.

2 In a large bowl, combine the carrots, onion, dates, and walnuts. Drizzle the dressing over the salad and toss to coat. Sprinkle with additional Aleppo pepper, if desired.

Chopped Salad

Serves 4

This is the most common salad you'll find on just about every menu in Israel, for breakfast, lunch, and dinner. So as a half-Israeli married to an Israeli, this is obviously a big part of our lives. We make it at least three or four times a week as a side to almost every meal we have, any time of day. There's no turning back with this salad; it's a friend for life. But while I love a classic, I like to play around with it, too, adding less traditional ingredients like dill or chopped fresh radishes. Here I've given you the classic plus a variation with Greek vibes that includes Kalamata olives and feta.

5 medium tomatoes

2 red bell peppers

5 Persian (mini) cucumbers

1 small red onion

½ cup chopped fresh parsley

½ cup chopped fresh dill (optional)

⅓ cup extra-virgin olive oil

Juice of 1 lemon

Kosher salt

1 Finely chop the tomatoes, bell peppers, cucumbers, and onion. As you chop, toss the vegetables into a colander to let some of their juices drain.

2 In a large bowl, combine the chopped vegetables with the parsley and dill (if using). Dress with the olive oil and lemon juice and toss thoroughly to combine. Season with salt to taste.

VARIATION

Greek-Style Chopped Salad

Add a handful of Kalamata olives and 1 large chunk of Bulgarian feta (crumbled, about ½ cup).

Tahini Caesar

Serves 2

This is clearly not a Middle Eastern classic, but I found myself wanting to add a Caesar regardless—probably because you can't live in the States and not love this creamy, garlicky salad and eat it on the regular. Ido and I are also obsessed with the Caesar-inspired romaine salad that Roberta's in Brooklyn does. So here is my version with my kind of twist, which features—can you guess?—tahini. Duh. I keep the lettuce leaves whole (which Roberta's does, too), so that you can eat the salad with your hands, which in my mind makes it taste even better. This salad plus Baharat Whole Roasted Chicken (page 211) and a fat glass of wine . . . it doesn't get much better than that.

Tahini Caesar Dressing

2 anchovy fillets

1 garlic clove

2 heaping tablespoons tahini paste

Juice of ½ lemon

1 tablespoon red wine vinegar

1 teaspoon Dijon mustard

⅓ cup extra-virgin olive oil

1 tablespoon ice water, plus more as needed

⅓ cup freshly grated Parmesan (I like a Microplane for this)

Kosher salt and freshly ground black pepper

Salad

1 cup raw walnuts

¼ cup honey or maple syrup

Kosher salt

2 heads of baby romaine or Little Gem lettuce, separated into leaves

3 radishes, sliced on a mandoline

⅔ cup freshly grated Parmesan (I like a Microplane for this), plus more for serving

Freshly ground black pepper

1 Preheat the oven to 350°F.

2 **Make the Tahini Caesar dressing:** Finely chop the anchovies and garlic together and transfer them to a medium bowl. Whisk in the tahini, lemon juice, vinegar, and mustard. While whisking, drizzle in the olive oil, followed by the ice water. Mix in the Parmesan and season with salt and pepper. If the dressing looks like it's separating or needs to be thinned out, whisk in a little more water until it emulsifies or reaches your ideal drizzling consistency.

3 **Make the salad:** On a baking sheet, toss together the walnuts, honey, and a pinch of salt. Bake until the walnuts are caramelized, 3 to 5 minutes. Let cool.

4 Arrange a layer of lettuce on a plate, drizzle over some of the dressing, and sprinkle with some of the caramelized walnuts, radishes, and grated cheese. Layer with another round of lettuce, walnuts, radishes, and cheese and keep going until it's done; that way you get dressing and toppings throughout the salad without having to toss. Finish with lots of cracked black pepper and grated Parm—load up that cheese, baby.

French Lentils with Beets, Sour Cherries, Urfa, and Almonds

Serves 4

I've always thought that lentils are such a powerful ingredient because of the way they instantly make any dish heartier. When tossed with tart dried cherries, honey-roasted beets, and an Urfa-spiked vinaigrette, they're the perfect base for a dish that's way more substantial than you'd ever think a salad could be. The beet method in the salad is swiped from the Vinegar and Honey–Roasted Beets (page 110), so if you have those left over, use them here.

Salad

3 small beets, well scrubbed

1½ tablespoons red wine vinegar

1½ tablespoons honey

1½ strips of orange zest

½ teaspoon coriander seeds

1½ teaspoons kosher salt

1 cup French lentils, rinsed

1 bunch of fresh cilantro, finely chopped

1 shallot, finely chopped

1 cup chopped toasted almonds

⅓ cup dried sour cherries, chopped

Dressing

1 tablespoon honey

2 teaspoons red wine vinegar

Grated zest of 1 lemon

Juice of ½ lemon, plus more to taste

½ garlic clove, minced

1½ teaspoons kosher salt, plus more to taste

½ teaspoon Urfa or Aleppo pepper or chili flakes

¼ teaspoon freshly ground black pepper

¼ cup extra-virgin olive oil

1 **Make the salad:** Preheat the oven to 350°F.

2 In a medium bowl, combine the beets, vinegar, honey, orange zest, coriander seeds, ½ teaspoon of the salt, and ½ tablespoon water. Toss to coat. Arrange the beets on a rimmed baking sheet and cover the tray tightly with foil. Roast until the beets can be easily pierced with a knife and the skin starts to caramelize, about 45 minutes. Remove the foil and swirl the beets in the sticky sauce to coat. Once the beets are cool enough to handle, cut them into ½-inch chunks. (Yep, the skin says on—so tasty with all that sweet glaze!)

3 Meanwhile, rinse the lentils under cold water. Place them in a medium pot with 2½ cups water and the remaining 1 teaspoon salt. Bring to a boil over high heat, reduce to a simmer, and cover. Cook the lentils over medium-low heat until they are tender but not mushy, about 20 minutes. Drain well and allow to cool slightly.

4 In a large bowl, toss together the lentils, beets, cilantro, shallot, almonds, and cherries.

5 **Make the dressing:** In a medium bowl, whisk together the honey, vinegar, lemon zest, lemon juice, garlic, salt, Urfa, and black pepper. Continue whisking as you stream in the olive oil. Whisk until the dressing is emulsified, about 1 minute. Taste and adjust the seasoning with more lemon juice and/or salt.

6 Drizzle the dressing over the salad, toss to coat, and serve.

Watermelon Salad with Feta, Pepitas, and Mint

Serves 6

Growing up—and pretty much every summer in Tel Aviv since—we'd always have fresh watermelon with creamy Bulgarian cheese as a beach snack. It's the perfect combination of juicy, sweet, and salty, which only gets better with the Mexican twist I give it, adding vibrant lime, pumpkin seeds, and chile (in this case, Aleppo). This salad is bound to be your new summer staple—it's perfect at any BBQ or for eating on the beach in nothing but a bathing suit.

8 cups sliced watermelon (from about 1 small watermelon)

1 cup crumbled sheep's milk feta (Bulgarian, if you can find it)

Grated zest and juice of 1 lime

1 teaspoon Aleppo pepper or red chile flakes

¼ cup pumpkin seeds, toasted in a dry pan until fragrant

⅓ cup fresh mint leaves, larger leaves torn in half

Arrange the sliced watermelon on a large serving platter and scatter the feta over the top, along with the lime zest and juice. Sprinkle with the Aleppo and pumpkin seeds and finish with the fresh mint.

Dad's Sunday Brunch Salad

Serves 6

I have no idea where he got the recipe from, but this is one of the signature dishes my dad cooks (his tool of choice for cutting the tomatoes: a steak knife). There's not much more to it than chopped tomatoes (an assortment of the ripest in-season varieties) and a ton of olive oil and vinegar—and anyone who's had it will tell you that it's just about perfect. If we were having Sunday brunch—and we were always having Sunday brunch—then a big bowl of this was on the table alongside the smoked salmon, chubs, herring, cheeses, and fresh bagels. It's just one of those really delicious, simple, light salads that you can't get sick of.

6 medium tomatoes, thinly sliced

2 cups cherry tomatoes, halved

6 spring onions or scallions, thinly sliced

1 cup chopped fresh cilantro

1 garlic clove, grated

2 tablespoons extra-virgin olive oil

1 tablespoon balsamic vinegar

Kosher salt and freshly ground black pepper

In a large bowl, combine the tomatoes, onions, cilantro, and garlic. Dress with the olive oil and vinegar and season with salt to taste and a ton of pepper—just the way Dad does it.

Handheld
Meals

I'm all about a casual meal, especially one that's best enjoyed hunkered over the sink—

no plate or chair required. Even more of a bonus if it can be made mostly out of components I already have lying around—or that I can repurpose for future meals if I do have to do some cooking. Either way, these sandwiches, toasts, and flatbreads are a quintessential feature of Middle Eastern and Mediterranean eating, where—let's be honest—you haven't really had a meal if you haven't had bread. Just about anything is better with it, whether you're schmearing, dipping, spreading, and sopping, or layering everything up for the perfect bite.

Sabich with Fried Eggplant, Seven-Minute Eggs, and Chopped Salad

Serves 4

This is probably one of the most popular pita sandwiches in Israel, and it's a vegetarian's dream. There's fried eggplant layered with pickled mango amba, Garlicky Tahini, boiled potato, and a bright, fresh veg salad. Then instead of the traditional hard-boiled egg, I call for my more softly boiled seven-minute version. All that creamy egg yolk getting in the mix? Forget it. You won't miss the meat.

2 small or 1 medium eggplant, cut into ½-inch-thick slices

Kosher salt

Grapeseed oil, for shallow-frying

4 Easy Peasy Pitas (page 150) or store-bought (the fluffiest you can find)

4 Seven-Minute Eggs (page 52), halved (or you could scramble the eggs)

1 cup Chopped Salad (page 114)

Garlicky Tahini (page 37), for serving

Amba (see page 22), for serving

Green Zhug (page 50), for serving

Fresh parsley, for serving

NOTE *Everything in this pita eats really well as a salad. Use the chopped salad as a base and top it with the eggplant, egg, tahini, amba, and parsley. It's an amazing gluten-free option or just a sick lunch.*

1 Lay the eggplant slices on a layer of paper towels. Generously sprinkle salt over the top of the slices and let them sit until the eggplant starts to "sweat" out its water, 20 to 30 minutes. Blot thoroughly with fresh paper towels.

2 In a large skillet, heat about ¼ inch oil over medium-high heat until it shimmers. Working in batches so you don't crowd the pan, fry the eggplant until golden brown, 3 to 4 minutes per side. Transfer the eggplant to a plate lined with paper towels. Add more oil to the pan if it starts to get dry; eggplant soaks it up like a sponge.

3 Stuff each pita with some fried eggplant, an egg, ¼ cup chopped salad, a drizzle of garlicky tahini, plus a dollop of amba and green zhug. Sprinkle with the parsley and dig in.

Tomato–Mustard Seed Jam and Za'atar Toast

Serves 6 to 8

I'm all for letting heat do the work for me, and this tomato jam is the perfect example of that kind of lazy-but-amazing cooking. You let the tomatoes cook—skin on (because, lazy)—low and slow so they completely melt down, becoming tangy, tart, and sweet. I love spreading the jam on toast, maybe topped with a fried egg or different cheeses, and definitely a drizzle of tahini plus a sprinkle of za'atar, which kinda gives you pizza vibes.

2 tablespoons extra-virgin olive oil

2 teaspoons black mustard seeds

1 large yellow onion, finely chopped

10 medium tomatoes, roughly chopped

1 tablespoon honey

1 teaspoon kosher salt

6 to 8 pieces sourdough bread, toasted

Za'atar, store-bought or homemade (see page 31), for serving

Tahini (optional), store-bought or homemade (see page 37), for serving

1 In a large saucepan, heat the oil over medium heat. Add the mustard seeds and cook just until they start to pop, about 3 minutes. Add the onion and cook, stirring occasionally, until translucent, 3 to 5 minutes. Add the tomatoes, honey, and salt and stir to combine. Reduce the heat to medium-low, cover, and cook until saucy, 5 to 10 minutes. Remove the lid and continue cooking until the liquid evaporates and the mixture becomes sticky and jammy, about 40 minutes.

2 Smear on sourdough toast and top with a sprinkle of za'atar and a drizzle of tahini (if using).

Avocado Za'atar Barbari

Serves 2

You might be looking at this and thinking we're getting kinda basic, but avocados are really freaking good in Israel, so when I'm there, I'm always bringing them home from the market by the armful and layering them over good, fresh bread. This version takes the idea up a notch by layering the avocado with fresh radish, pickled red onion, cilantro (or whatever fresh herbs you like, for any cilantro-haters), and a gorgeous green hot sauce. But the best part by far is the salty, doughy bread, which is a Persian-inspired recipe that is really easy to make at home and takes your toast game to a whole new level.

1 large or 2 small Za'atar
   Nan-e Barbari (page 147)

2 avocados, sliced

Green Zhug (page 50)
   or sliced jalapeño

Sliced radishes

Quick-Pickled Red Onion
   (page 57)

Cilantro leaves or other fresh
   herb leaves

½ lemon

Extra-virgin olive oil

Coarse sea salt

Freshly ground black pepper

Top the flatbread with the avocado slices, followed by the zhug, radishes, pickled red onion, and cilantro leaves. Squeeze the lemon over the flatbreads, drizzle with olive oil, and sprinkle with sea salt and black pepper to serve.

Sesame Schnitzel Sandwich with Harissa Honey and Tartar Slaw

Serves 4

Everyone should have a schnitzel recipe in their back pocket. It's (a) the perfect way to release all your anger while pounding the chicken thin (it's a great "I'm pissed at the world but I'm going to make myself something delicious" meal), and (b) a total family-pleaser. What kid doesn't like some kind of crispy chicken dish? Forget that—what adult is going to turn down perfectly golden fried chicken mounded with creamy slaw?! It's my Middle Eastern take on a good ol' American fried chicken sandwich.

Chicken Schnitzel

4 boneless, skinless chicken breasts, butterflied

4 large eggs

Kosher salt

1 cup all-purpose flour

Freshly ground black pepper

2 cups panko bread crumbs, pulsed in a blender until fine

1 cup sesame seeds

Grapeseed oil, for shallow-frying

Tartar Slaw

1 cup mayonnaise

3 tablespoons finely chopped fresh dill

1 tablespoon capers, drained and finely chopped

1 tablespoon finely chopped pickle (I love Israeli pickles, but any garlicky variety will work)

1 tablespoon Dijon mustard

2 teaspoons fresh lemon juice

1 teaspoon white wine vinegar

Kosher salt and freshly ground black pepper

½ head of red cabbage, finely sliced

Assembly

2 tablespoons Harissa (page 46) or store-bought

2 tablespoons honey

4 brioche buns, potato buns, or pita, split and lightly toasted

Butter lettuce leaves

1 radish (regular, watermelon, or purple), very thinly sliced (use a mandoline if you have one)

1 Prepare the chicken schnitzel: Place the butterflied chicken breasts between two sheets of parchment or plastic wrap and use a rolling pin or skillet to pound them out until each is ¼ inch thick. Then cut each cutlet in half.

2 Set up a breading station: In a shallow bowl, beat the eggs with a pinch of salt. Place the flour in a second shallow bowl and season with salt and pepper. In a third, mix together the panko, sesame seeds, and salt and pepper to taste. Working with one piece at a time, place the chicken cutlets in the flour, dust off any excess, then dredge through the beaten egg. Let any excess drip off before placing the chicken in the panko-sesame mixture. Gently press the panko onto the chicken to ensure it's well coated. Transfer to a plate.

3 In a large skillet, heat about ½ inch grapeseed oil over medium-high heat until it shimmers. Add 2 or 3 pieces of chicken (as many as you can fit without overcrowding the pan) and fry until crispy and golden, 2 to 3 minutes per side. Transfer the chicken to a wire cooling rack, immediately seasoning it with salt. Repeat with the remaining chicken pieces as necessary.

4 Make the tartar slaw: In a large bowl, whisk together the mayo, dill, capers, pickle, mustard, lemon juice, vinegar, and a pinch each of salt and pepper. Taste for seasoning and adjust as desired. Add the cabbage and massage the sauce in with your hands, ensuring the cabbage is totally coated and beginning to soften.

5 To assemble: In a small bowl, mix together the harissa and honey. On each bun, build a sandwich with a leaf of butter lettuce, 2 pieces of the crispy chicken schnitzel, a drizzle of harissa honey, a scoop of the tartar slaw, and a few slices of radish.

Pita Grilled Cheese with Gouda and Honey

Serves 2

Ido and I both have really fond childhood memories of eating cheesy toasts in Israel—just toasted sesame bread topped with a mild white cheese that would get stringy and delicious. Here, I fancied it up a bit with some nigella and sesame seeds and finished it with a little honey for some of that sweet-salty goodness. But if you wanted to scrap all that and just go for cheese in a pita? No one's gonna be mad at a grilled cheese.

2 cups shredded Gouda

2 tablespoons sesame seeds, plus more for serving

1 tablespoon plus 1 teaspoon nigella seeds, plus more for serving

3 tablespoons unsalted butter, at room temperature

2 Easy Peasy Pitas (page 150) or store-bought (the fluffiest you can find)

Honey, for serving

1 In a medium bowl, toss together the Gouda, sesame seeds, and nigella seeds. Using a serrated knife, slice a corner off each pita and open up the pocket. If it doesn't open easily, use a sharp knife to gently slice through the middle, creating a pocket. Butter the inside and outside of each pita and stuff them with the cheese mixture.

2 Heat a medium skillet over medium heat. Arrange the pitas in the warm skillet and press down with a spatula. Toast until the first side of the bread is lightly golden, 5 to 7 minutes. Flip and repeat on the other side, 5 to 7 minutes.

3 Cut each pita in half and drizzle with honey and sprinkle over more seeds. Serve hot.

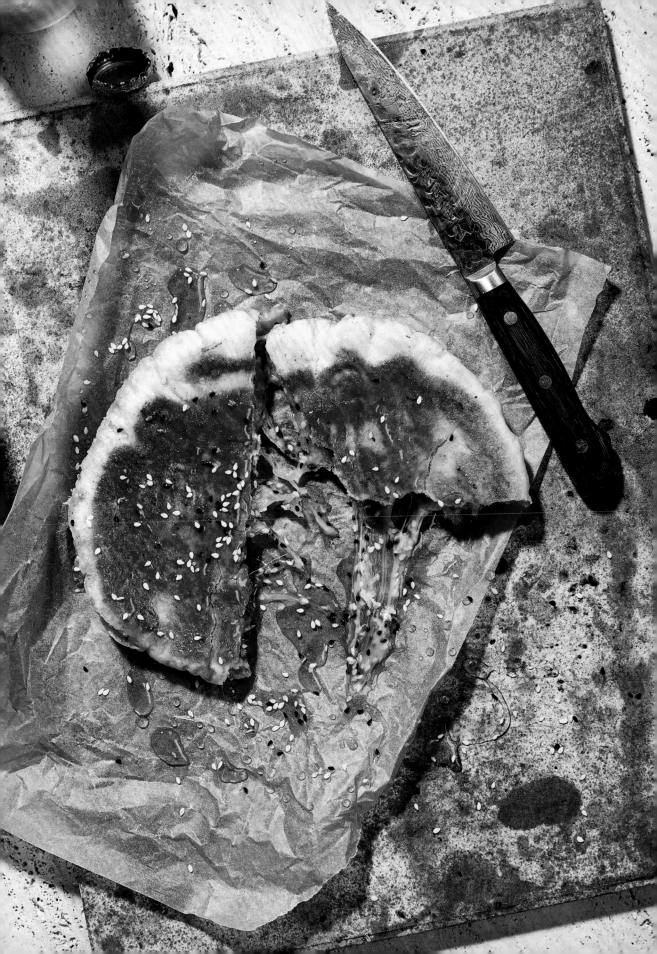

Beef Kebab Burgers with Garlicky Tahini and Red Zhug

Serves 4

There are many variations of kebab around the world, but when I think of kebab, ground meat seasoned to perfection, grilled on a skewer, and served with lots of Garlicky Tahini is what comes to mind. I'm turning things up a little by forming the same mixture into a patty that I can cook up just like a big, juicy burger and top with my favorite fixin's—pickled onions, Garlicky Tahini, and red zhug. It tastes exactly like the pita sandwiches that I regularly take down on the streets of Tel Aviv.

Burgers

1 pound ground beef (85% lean) or lamb

¼ cup finely chopped red onion

¼ cup chopped fresh parsley

¼ cup chopped fresh mint

2 tablespoons pine nuts, toasted in a dry pan until fragrant

2 garlic cloves, minced

1 teaspoon kosher salt, plus more to taste

½ teaspoon ground cumin

¼ teaspoon freshly ground black pepper, plus more to taste

Pinch of ground cinnamon

2 tablespoons extra-virgin olive oil (optional; for pan-searing the burgers)

Assembly

4 brioche or potato buns, split and lightly toasted

Garlicky Tahini (page 37)

Red Zhug (page 50)

Quick-Pickled Red Onion (page 57)

1 Persian (mini) cucumber, thinly sliced

2 radishes, thinly sliced

Chopped fresh parsley

1 **Make the burgers:** In a large bowl, combine the beef, onion, parsley, mint, pine nuts, garlic, salt, cumin, pepper, and cinnamon. Mix thoroughly to combine. Evenly divide the mixture into 4 patties, roughly 1 inch thick. Season the outsides of the patties with more salt and pepper (I love a salty crust on my burgers).

2 Preheat the grill until hot. (Or to pan-sear the burgers, heat the olive oil in a cast-iron skillet over medium-high heat.) Add the burgers to the grill (or pan) and sear for about 3 minutes, until a nice char has formed. Flip and cook for another 4 minutes for medium, or until done to your liking. Let the patties rest for 5 minutes before building the burgers.

3 **Assemble the burgers:** On each bun, spread some garlicky tahini followed by a little zhug, then a burger. Top with pickled onions, cucumber, radishes, and a sprinkling of parsley. Schmear a little more garlicky tahini on the top and close.

Handheld Meals

Easy Chicken Shawarma in a Pita

Serves 6

Shawarma is one of the most popular street foods in the Middle East, and I've found that it's really easy to make a pretty damn delicious version in your own kitchen. It first takes marinating some chicken thighs for as long as you can (ideally overnight). The thighs are my favorite part of the bird because they pack the most flavor, stay juiciest the longest, and need very little to taste amazing. Sear the thighs, then tuck them into the fluffiest, freshest pitas you can find (please, please, please give the ones on page 150 a shot). And definitely try to have amba on hand—it gives this pita that authentic shawarma flavor.

Chicken

6 boneless, skinless chicken thighs

3 to 5 tablespoons extra-virgin olive oil (the larger amount if pan-searing the chicken)

3 garlic cloves, grated

1 tablespoon Shawarma Spice Blend (page 184) or store-bought

Kosher salt and freshly ground black pepper

Assembly

6 Easy Peasy Pitas (page 150) or store-bought

1 cup Garlicky Tahini (page 37)

Green Zhug (page 50)

Amba (see page 22)

2 cups Chopped Salad (page 114)

Quick-Pickled Red Onion (page 57)

Chopped fresh parsley

1 Make the chicken: In a large bowl, combine the chicken thighs, 3 tablespoons of the olive oil, the garlic, and the shawarma spice blend. Place in the fridge and marinate for at least 2 hours and up to overnight. Let the chicken come to room temperature for 1 hour before cooking. Remove the chicken from the bowl, discarding the marinade, and season well with salt and pepper.

2 Preheat a grill until hot. (Or to pan-sear, heat the remaining 2 tablespoons oil in a large skillet over medium-high heat.) Grill (or pan-sear) the chicken until cooked through and just crisp or lightly charred, about 5 minutes per side. Slice each thigh into strips.

3 There is a proper method to stuffing a pita, and here it is: Lay the pita on its side so that when you layer the ingredients they are getting spread evenly—ensuring you get a taste of everything in each bite. Schmear one side of the inside of the pita with tahini, followed by zhug, a little amba, some of the salad, then the sliced chicken. Place pickled red onion on top, plus a little more salad to fill in any empty space in the pita. Finish with more tahini, zhug, amba, and some parsley.

Lamb Flatbread with Pomegranate and Mint

Dough for Nan-e Barbari
(page 146)

Lamb Topping

2 pounds ground lamb

1 medium red onion,
finely diced

2 garlic cloves, grated

1 teaspoon ground coriander

1 teaspoon ground cumin

1 teaspoon Aleppo pepper,
cayenne pepper, chili
powder, or Urfa pepper

½ teaspoon ground turmeric

Pinch of ground cinnamon

Kosher salt and freshly
ground black pepper

2 cups chopped tomatoes

¼ cup pomegranate
molasses

All-purpose flour, for dusting

Serving

Fresh pomegranate seeds

Torn fresh mint leaves

Sumac

Labneh (page 52) or Lemony
Yogurt (page 56)

NOTE *This recipe makes
2 large flatbreads to serve 8.
If you want to make only 1 (to
serve 4 people), make the full
amount of dough, wrap half
of it in plastic wrap, and store
it in the fridge up to overnight
for another batch the next
day. Then just halve the
topping ingredients here.*

Serves 8 (see Note)

I'm such a big fan of Nan-e Barbari (page 146) as a vehicle
for all things saucy and delicious that I wanted to use it
as a base for my version of *lahmacun*, a Turkish-style
pizza. The combination of the rich lamb plus pops of fresh
pomegranate is sweet-savory heaven. I love serving this
with cold, creamy labneh or lemony yogurt—it's a crucial
tangy element to offset the richness of the flatbread.

1 Make the dough as directed through the first rise.

2 Preheat the oven to 500°F. Place a pizza stone or an
overturned baking sheet on the lowest possible rack to
preheat.

3 **Make the lamb topping:** Heat a large skillet over
medium-high heat and cook the lamb, breaking it up
with the back of a wooden spoon, until browned, about
7 minutes. Add the onion, garlic, coriander, cumin,
Aleppo pepper, turmeric, and cinnamon. Season with salt
and black pepper to taste and cook until the spices are
fragrant and the onion softens slightly, 1 to 2 minutes.

4 Add the tomatoes and cook, mashing gently with the
back of a wooden spoon, until the tomatoes break down
and get saucy with the ground meat, 10 to 15 minutes.
Remove the pan from the heat and stir in the pomegranate
molasses. Set aside to cool while you shape the dough.

5 Line two baking sheets with parchment paper and
lightly dust with flour. Set aside.

6 Punch down the dough and turn it out onto a floured
surface. Divide the dough into 2 large pieces. Use a rolling
pin to roll each piece into an oblong shape ¼ to ½ inch
thick. Place one piece on each of the prepared baking
sheets. Cover each with a clean towel and and allow the
dough to proof for 20 minutes.

7 Divide the lamb mixture between the 2 flatbreads and
spread it out in an even layer, leaving as much room for the
crust as you like. Press the topping in with your fingers,
making little dents. Transfer one of the flatbreads and
parchment directly onto the preheated pizza stone or
baking sheet and bake until the crust is lightly browned,
about 10 minutes. Repeat with the second flatbread.

8 **To serve:** Sprinkle each flatbread with pomegranate
seeds, mint, and a nice pinch of sumac. Serve with labneh
or lemony yogurt.

Turmeric–Black Pepper Malawach

Serves 6

Malawach is a pancake-like Yemeni flatbread that gets super flaky and crispy thanks to the butter in the dough. It's traditionally served with a grated tomato dip and hard-boiled eggs, but I've given this a little update by working turmeric and black pepper into the dough, then topping it with a light tomato salsa and a custardy, jammy egg.

Malawach
4 cups all-purpose flour

2 tablespoons sugar

2 teaspoons kosher salt

1 teaspoon ground turmeric

¼ teaspoon freshly ground black pepper

8 tablespoons (1 stick) salted butter, at room temperature, plus more for generously greasing your hands and work surface

Pico de Gallo
2 medium tomatoes, chopped

Small handful of cilantro, stems and leaves, roughly chopped

½ serrano pepper, finely chopped (if you want it spicier, keep the seeds in)

1 tablespoon chopped red onion

½ garlic clove, grated

½ teaspoon kosher salt

Serving
6 Seven-Minute Eggs (page 52)

Flaky sea salt and freshly ground black pepper

Garlicky Tahini (page 37)

NOTE *The longer the tomatoes sit on the* malawach, *the more quickly it will lose its crispness, so plate right before you eat. Or, if you're serving a big group, serve everything separate and let people assemble their own.*

1 **Make the malawach:** In a large bowl, whisk together the flour, sugar, kosher salt, turmeric, and black pepper. Add 1½ cups water, working it in with your hands until the dough comes together, about 3 minutes. If the dough seems too dry and crumbly, add more water, 1 tablespoon at a time. Knead the dough for 5 minutes, until it feels smooth and springy. Wrap in plastic wrap and refrigerate for at least 1 hour.

2 Line a baking sheet with parchment paper and set aside. Unwrap the dough and cut it into 6 equal pieces. Generously grease your hands and a clean work surface with butter; this will make it easier to handle the dough and will allow you to roll it out as thin as possible without tearing it. Use your hands to gently roll each piece into a ball. Working with one at a time, begin flattening the dough against the work surface with your hands. Continue pulling and stretching out the dough until it is quite thin, to the point that you can see the counter underneath—be gentle and work slowly! The dough should be very elastic, so it shouldn't break easily. Spread 1 teaspoon of the butter over the stretched-out dough. Roll up the sheet of dough into a long rope, then coil it around itself like a snail shell. Place it on the prepared baking sheet under a clean kitchen towel or sheet of plastic wrap to rest as you prep the remaining dough. When you're done, tightly cover the baking sheet with plastic wrap and refrigerate for at least 1 hour or overnight. (I like to do this a day in advance.)

3 Remove the *malawach* from the fridge. In a large skillet over medium heat, melt 1 tablespoon of the butter. Working with one at a time, use a rolling pin to roll out a *malawach* until it's ⅛ inch thick and place it in the pan. Cook for about 2 minutes per side, until crispy. Repeat to cook the remaining *malawach,* using 1 tablespoon butter for each one.

4 **Make the pico de gallo:** In a medium bowl, toss together the tomatoes, cilantro, serrano, onion, garlic, and kosher salt.

5 **To serve:** After cooking the seven-minute eggs, peel and halve them and season with sea salt and black pepper to taste. Top each warm *malawach* with a spoonful of the pico and an egg. Drizzle with garlicky tahini and serve (see Note).

Nan-e Barbari (Persian Flatbread)

Makes 2 large or 4 small flatbreads

Toronto is one of the most multicultural cities in the world, and my dad always made a point of introducing us to new and interesting foods. One of our favorite places to go was (and still is) a Persian grocery store, where they make fresh *nan-e barbari,* a flatbread brushed with a glaze and flecked with earthy, nutty nigella seeds, that we'd eat straight from the oven. Any we managed to bring home would get packed up in our lunches or served with dinner, but those first doughy, steamy bites were pure magic. I knew I needed to come up with my own (slightly less traditional) version—no glaze, finishing with olive oil instead—not only because it's insanely delicious but also because it's so versatile with the toppings you can add to it. I came up with three variations that play around with different spices: nigella, the OG *barbari*; za'atar and olive oil, inspired by the flatbreads I get in the markets in Israel; and then sesame seeds and sea salt, a classic combination that brings great depth and dimension to whatever you put it on.

I promise you're going to be able to pull off something really special when you make this at home. If need be, you can make the dough the night before and then let it slowly proof overnight. Either way, be sure to let your oven get really, really hot. Like seriously hot.

1 envelope (2¼ teaspoons) active dry yeast

¼ cup sugar

4½ cups bread flour, plus more for dusting

2 tablespoons grapeseed oil

1 tablespoon kosher salt

⅓ cup extra-virgin olive oil

Flaky sea salt

1 In a stand mixer, whisk together the yeast and sugar with 2¼ cups warm water (not hot or you'll kill the yeast!). Let the mixture sit until the yeast has gotten nice and frothy, about 5 minutes. Attach the dough hook, add the flour and grapeseed oil, and mix for 5 minutes. Sprinkle in the kosher salt and mix for another 5 minutes. The dough may be a little shaggy, but don't be tempted to overmix. Cover the bowl with plastic wrap and set it in a warm place until the dough doubles in size, about 1 hour. (The inside of your oven is always a good bet—just make sure it's not on! I also like bringing the bowl into the bathroom when I take a shower. Such a lovely, warm place to bloom!) If baking the next day, after 1 hour of proofing, cover the bowl in plastic wrap and refrigerate overnight. Remove from the refrigerator and let the dough come to room temperature before proceeding to step 2. The dough will be a little more proofed, but that's okay.

2 Line two baking sheets with parchment paper and lightly dust with flour. Set aside.

3 Preheat the oven to 500°F. Place a pizza stone or an overturned baking sheet on the lowest rack to preheat.

4 Punch down the dough and turn it out onto a floured surface. Divide the dough into 2 large pieces or 4 smaller ones. Use a rolling pin to roll each piece into an oblong shape ¼ to ½ inch thick. Place each piece on a prepared baking sheet. Cover the dough with a damp towel and allow it to proof again for 30 minutes.

5 Brush the dough with the olive oil to coat. Using the tips of your fingers, make a series of lengthwise indentations down the dough, about 1 inch apart. Add any desired toppings and sprinkle with sea salt.

6 Working one at a time, lift the parchment with the dough on top and place it directly onto the preheated stone or baking sheet. Bake until the bread is golden on all sides, about 5 minutes. Transfer the bread to the baking rack and let it cool before serving. Repeat with the remaining dough.

VARIATIONS

Nigella-Sesame Nan-e Barbari

After brushing the dough with olive oil and making the indentations, sprinkle all over with ¼ cup nigella seeds and ¼ cup sesame seeds. Season with sea salt.

Za'atar Nan-e Barbari

Mix ¼ cup za'atar (homemade [page 31] or store-bought) with the original recipe's ⅓ cup olive oil and slather it over the dough instead of brushing, making sure some seeps into the little trenches as you make the indentations. Season with sea salt.

Sesame Nan-e Barbari

After brushing the dough with olive oil and making the indentations, sprinkle all over with ½ cup sesame seeds and season with sea salt.

Easy Peasy Pita

Makes 12 pitas

Pita is the perfect delivery system for food—it's soft and doughy yet strong enough for scooping and dipping, or you can stuff it like a sandwich and not lose any of the juices that seep out. Genius. I know that making your own pita sounds a little hardcore, but I promise that this recipe is easy-peasy, and it's here because store-bought pita can be kinda meh (and when I say meh, I mean crap).

1 envelope (2¼ teaspoons) active dry yeast

1½ tablespoons sugar

1½ tablespoons extra-virgin olive oil

5 cups all-purpose flour, plus more for dusting

1 tablespoon kosher salt

NOTE *If your pita doesn't have a pocket, that's okay! Just slice off a small piece from the side and carefully slide a serrated knife inside to create a pocket—ideally without slicing all the way through. But if it does break in half, no sweat; it'll still mop up hummus beautifully.*

1 In a stand mixer, whisk together the yeast, sugar, and 1 cup warm (not hot) water. Let sit for 5 minutes, until the mixture is foamy. In a separate medium bowl, combine 1 cup water and the olive oil.

2 Attach the dough hook to the stand mixer. Add the flour to the yeast mixture and mix on low speed. Right away, add the olive oil/water mixture and continue mixing for 5 minutes. Add the salt and increase the speed to medium-low, mixing for another 5 minutes. The dough will be on the wet side but everything should be incorporated. If you need to, scrape the bottom of the bowl with a spatula to make sure all the ingredients are getting pulled into the dough. Cover the dough with plastic wrap and let it double in size in a warm place, about 1 hour 30 minutes.

3 Cut 12 roughly 5-inch squares out of parchment paper and lightly dust them with flour. Then lightly dust a clean work surface and your hands with flour. Break off a tennis ball–size piece of dough and loosely form it into a ball. Using a well-floured rolling pin, roll the ball to about ¼ inch thick and place it on one of the prepared parchment squares. Cover with a clean towel as you continue rolling out the remaining pita. Let the dough proof at room temperature for 1 hour to 1 hour 30 minutes, depending on how warm the room is.

4 About 30 minutes before baking, place a pizza stone or an overturned baking sheet on the lowest rack, make sure nothing else is in the oven. Preheat the oven to 500°F.

5 Line a bowl or basket with a kitchen towel and have it at the ready. Working with 2 at a time, carefully place the pita directly onto the pizza stone or baking sheet without taking it off the parchment (or it will lose air and its shape). Bake until puffed and flip over, 3 to 5 minutes total. You want it to be lightly toasted without much color, so be sure to keep an eye on it.

6 Using tongs, transfer the baked pita to the towel-lined bowl or basket and cover with another towel to keep warm as you finish baking the remaining pita.

7 Serve warm or let the pita cool before storing them in a plastic bag. Reheat them in the oven or toaster before serving.

All the Seeds Challah

Makes 2 loaves

Breads Bakery, an incredible Israeli bakeshop, makes an insane, larger-than-life challah that's essentially meant to be a centerpiece on your table—I mean, it has little ceramic bowls *braided into the freakin' challah* so it can be served with honey, sea salt, and butter. But my favorite part is that it's sprinkled with tons of seeds, like nigella, pumpkin, flax, sesame, and sunflower. I love how they add different textures, every bite gives you different flavors, and visually, it's just stunning. So this is my homage to the guys at Breads. Don't get too hung up on your braiding skills—it doesn't have to be perfect! I sometimes use the slightly more complicated four-strand braid, but the simple three-strand method will get you a gorgeous-looking challah. And the lusciously soft bread combined with the seeds and spices (I add za'atar to my mix) is going to be a crowd-pleaser no matter what.

2 envelopes (4½ teaspoons) active dry yeast

½ cup plus 1 teaspoon sugar

6¼ cups all-purpose flour, plus more for kneading

3 large eggs

3 large egg yolks

⅓ cup grapeseed oil, plus more for greasing

2½ tablespoons kosher salt

Egg wash: 1 egg yolk whisked with 1 tablespoon water

⅓ cup pumpkin seeds

2 tablespoons poppy seeds

2 tablespoons nigella seeds

2 tablespoons sesame seeds

2 tablespoons za'atar, store-bought or homemade (see page 31)

1 teaspoon flaky sea salt

1 In a medium bowl, dissolve the yeast and 1 teaspoon of the sugar in 1½ cups warm (not hot) water. Set aside for 5 minutes, until foamy.

2 In a stand mixer fitted with the dough hook, combine the flour, the remaining ½ cup sugar, the whole eggs, egg yolks, grapeseed oil, and kosher salt. Add the yeast mixture and mix on low speed for 10 to 15 minutes. It will still be a little sticky, and that's okay. Turn out the dough on a floured surface and sprinkle it with a little flour. Knead the dough for 5 minutes, sprinkling it with more flour if necessary to keep it from getting sticky, until the dough comes together and springs back when you touch it. Lightly coat a clean bowl with grapeseed oil and place the dough inside. Cover with plastic wrap and let the dough double in size in a warm place, 1 hour to 1 hour 30 minutes.

3 Line two baking sheets with parchment paper or silicone baking mats.

4 Remove the dough from the bowl and break it into 2 even pieces. Keep one piece under a towel while you work on braiding the other.

(recipe continues)

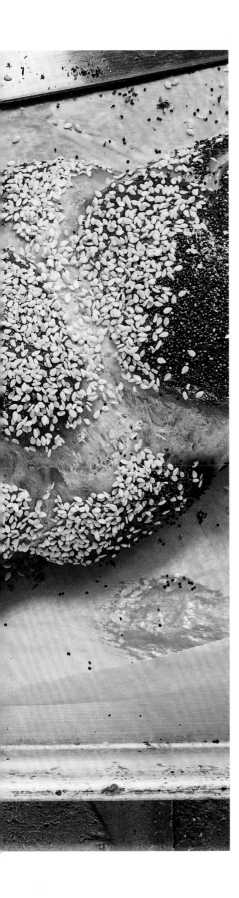

5 We're going to go with a simple 3-strand braid here: Break the piece of dough you're working with into 3 even pieces. Roll out each into a nice long rope about 1½ inches thick. Place the strands parallel on one of the prepared baking sheets, about 1 inch apart. At one end, gather up the ends of the ropes and gently press them together—this will hold your challah together as you braid. Begin braiding by lifting the piece on the right and passing it over the center piece. (So the piece that had been on the right is now in the center.) Take the piece on the left and pass it over the center piece. Continue in this pattern, trying to keep the braid as tight as possible. When you've gotten to the bottom of the ropes, pinch the ends together and gently tuck them under the loaf. Cover the dough with a damp towel. Repeat for the second loaf of challah. Let them proof in a warm place for 45 minutes to 1 hour, until the loaves have almost doubled in size.

6 Preheat the oven to 350°F.

7 When both loaves have proofed, brush them with the egg wash. Generously sprinkle the pumpkin, poppy, nigella, and sesame seeds and the za'atar over the loaves. (I like doing mine in a diagonal pattern.) Sprinkle the sea salt over the top.

8 Bake until the top of the challah gets nice and golden (but not too dark or it'll dry out) and feels hard when tapped with your finger, 30 to 40 minutes. Transfer the loaves to a cooling rack and serve warm or at room temperature.

Making
Veg
the Star

I know I'm not the first to say it, but vegetables deserve to be at the center of a meal.

I have nothing against meat or fish, but there's something so special about beautiful produce that's been perfectly cooked and paired with the right balance of textures and flavors. In fact, you can cook vegetables like you do meat and end up with a dish that's just as sumptuous and robust. There's a time and a place for veg-forward dishes that are light and bright, where the ingredients have been preserved in their pure, virgin form. But these are not those dishes. Reach for these when you want to add deep flavor and heartiness to your meal, alongside meat or in place of it.

QUICK NOTE *If you're having trouble finding the vegetables called for in any of these dishes, then maybe that's not the dish to be making at that moment. The more seasonally you cook, the more certain produce will be available, and the better your end result is going to be.*

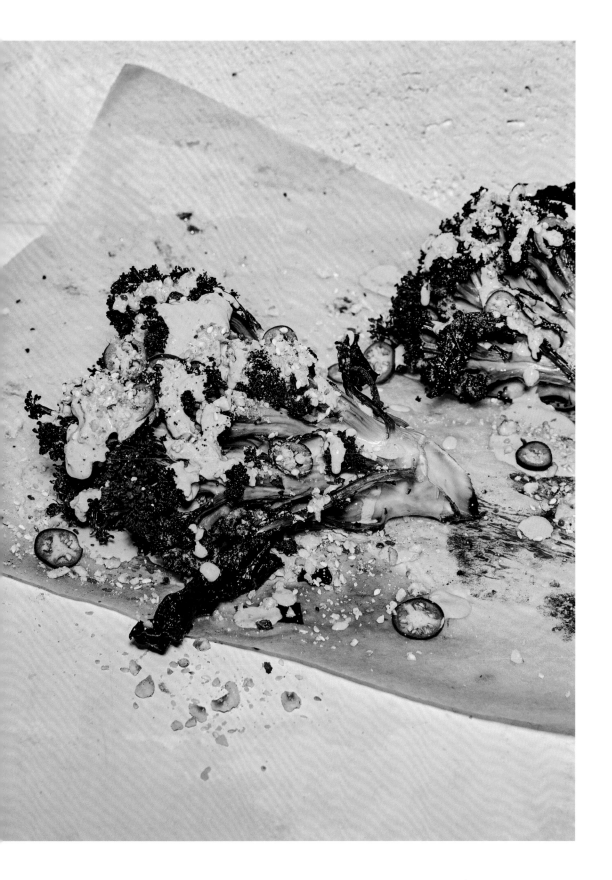

Sunchoke Rösti with Chive Sour Cream and Roasted Lemon

Serves 4

Sunchokes—or Jerusalem artichokes, as they're also known—are one of my favorite ingredients. They're like a little cheat because they have such incredible flavor that all they need is some acid and salt to taste delicious and complex—almost like an artichoke had a baby with a potato. I'm excited to use them here along with russet potatoes to ensure the rösti, which is basically a pan-size latke, gets extra crispy. (Though you could make these latke-size.) You could also substitute all potatoes if you can't find sunchokes, but they really do take this dish to a whole other place.

Chive Sour Cream

1 cup sour cream

½ cup finely chopped fresh chives

½ cup chopped fresh mint

1 teaspoon kosher salt

Roasted Lemon

1 lemon, very thinly sliced

1 tablespoon extra-virgin olive oil

Large pinch of kosher salt

Rösti

3 large sunchokes (about 1 pound)

2 medium russet potatoes

1 small yellow onion

3 large eggs, lightly beaten

2 heaping tablespoons all-purpose flour

2 teaspoons kosher salt

½ teaspoon freshly ground black pepper

4 tablespoons grapeseed oil

Serving

Freshly ground black pepper

Flaky sea salt

Fresh mint leaves

1 Make the chive sour cream: In a medium bowl, combine the sour cream, chives, mint, and kosher salt. Mix thoroughly and set aside.

2 Roast the lemon: Preheat the oven to 400°F.

3 Place the lemon slices in a single layer on a baking sheet, drizzle with the olive oil, and season with the kosher salt. Roast until lightly golden, about 5 minutes. Set aside.

4 Make the rösti: Wash and dry the sunchokes, then grate them into a medium bowl (no need to peel them). Peel the potatoes and grate them and the onion into the same bowl as the sunchokes. Transfer the grated mixture to a cheesecloth or clean kitchen towel and squeeze out all of the liquid. Really squeeze hard! The more moisture you can get out now, the crispier the rösti will be. In a medium bowl, mix together the squeezed-out sunchokes, potatoes, and onion with the eggs, flour, kosher salt, and pepper until thoroughly combined.

5 In a medium nonstick skillet, heat 2 tablespoons of the grapeseed oil over medium-high heat. Reduce the heat to medium-low and add half of the sunchoke mixture and press it down into the pan so it's in an even layer and really comes together. Fry until golden and crispy around the edges, 8 to 10 minutes. Carefully slide the rösti onto a large plate and flip the rösti back into the pan. Fry the second side until crisp, pressing down with a spatula as it cooks, another 5 minutes. When the rösti is done, slide it onto a plate and repeat with the remaining 2 tablespoons grapeseed oil and sunchoke mixture.

6 To serve: Cut the roasted lemon slices into quarters. Season the rösti with pepper and sea salt, then serve with the chive sour cream, fresh mint, and a sprinkle of the roasted lemon pieces.

A FEW NOTES *The sunchokes will oxidize, or turn brown, as you grate them—that's fine. Be sure to really squeeze out all the moisture so they're as dry as possible before frying. As for cooking, the name of the game here is low, slow, and crisp. You want the entire surface of the rösti to be equally caramelized and golden with crispy edges—don't rush it. Serve on a platter or garnish the rösti directly in the pan and bring it to the table as is.*

Honey-Roasted Parsnips with Dates and Tzatziki

Serves 4

I feel like parsnips don't get enough love. They're always taking a backseat to carrots, and I think it's time for that to change. Parsnips have the most incredible flavor that's just the right mix of earthy and sweet, and when you roast them with a little bit of honey at a high heat, you get a beautiful char that perfectly blends the two. (And yes, you can substitute carrots if you don't have parsnips on hand.) I serve them with sticky sweet dates on top of a pool of garlicky, tangy tzatziki to keep the dish light and playful.

Parsnips

6 medium parsnips or carrots, peeled and quartered lengthwise

3 tablespoons extra-virgin olive oil

1½ tablespoons honey

1 teaspoon Aleppo pepper

1½ teaspoons kosher salt

½ teaspoon ground coriander

¼ teaspoon ground turmeric

¼ teaspoon freshly ground black pepper

Tzatziki

1 cup whole-milk Greek yogurt

¼ cup chopped fresh dill

1 tablespoon fresh lemon juice

½ garlic clove, minced

½ teaspoon kosher salt, plus more to taste

Serving

6 Medjool dates, pitted and sliced

¼ cup hazelnuts, toasted and roughly chopped

Chopped fresh dill

Flaky sea salt

Extra-virgin olive oil

1 **Make the parsnips:** Preheat the oven to 450°F.

2 In a large bowl, combine the parsnips, olive oil, honey, Aleppo pepper, kosher salt, coriander, turmeric, and black pepper. Toss thoroughly to coat. Spread the mixture on a baking sheet and roast until tender and golden, about 25 minutes. Set aside.

3 **Make the tzatziki:** In a medium bowl, whisk together the yogurt, dill, lemon juice, garlic, and kosher salt. Taste and adjust for seasoning.

4 **To serve:** Evenly spread the tzatziki on a serving platter. Place the warm parsnips on top and garnish with the dates, hazelnuts, and a sprinkle of dill and sea salt. Finish with a drizzle of extra-virgin olive oil.

Grilled Summer Squash with Coriander Bread Crumbs

Serves 4

This dish is like a flavor bomb with vinegar-saturated squash that's been nicely not-quite-burnt so its smoky bitterness balances with garlicky, citrusy coriander-scented bread crumbs. Yes, I'm obsessed with coriander. And yes, you will be, too, after making this dish—it's just a magical spice that makes this incredibly simple dish a huge crowd-pleaser.

Squash

5 medium summer squash or zucchini or a combination (about 2½ pounds), cut lengthwise into ¼-inch-thick planks

2½ tablespoons extra-virgin olive oil

2 tablespoons white wine vinegar

Kosher salt and freshly ground black pepper

Bread Crumbs

2 teaspoons whole coriander seeds

3 tablespoons extra-virgin olive oil

1 garlic clove, grated

¾ cup panko bread crumbs, pulsed in a blender if chunkier crumbs

Kosher salt

Serving

Grated zest of 1 lemon

Extra-virgin olive oil

10 small fresh basil leaves (or 3 large ones, torn)

Flaky sea salt

1 **Make the squash:** Preheat the grill until it's hot. (Or preheat a large pan over medium-high heat.)

2 In a medium bowl, toss the squash with the olive oil, vinegar, and kosher salt and pepper to taste. Grill (or pan-sear) the squash on both sides until lightly charred, about 5 minutes total. (It will be about 1 minute per side in a pan.)

3 **Make the bread crumbs:** Toast the coriander in a dry pan until fragrant, about 30 seconds. Grind the seeds with a mortar and pestle or in a spice grinder. Heat the olive oil in a medium pan over medium heat. Add the garlic and cook for just 5 seconds, making sure it doesn't burn. Add the bread crumbs and season with kosher salt. Cook until the bread crumbs start to toast a bit, 3 to 5 minutes. Remove the pan from the heat and stir in the coriander.

4 **To serve:** Arrange the grilled squash on a serving plate and sprinkle the warm bread crumbs over the top. Finish with the lemon zest and a drizzle of olive oil, then scatter the basil over the top. Sprinkle with the sea salt.

Roasted Romanesco with Pistachios and Fried Caper Vinaigrette

Serves 4 as a side or 2 as a main

The food scene in Israel is constantly evolving, and it's a moment right now in which chefs are highlighting produce in its most natural form. That's exactly what I've done here with Romanesco, which isn't that common in Israel, but this cooking technique definitely is. Blanching it before roasting it whole (or halved, as I call for—for maximum surface area for caramelization) is key to ensuring a tender interior and sexy, charred exterior. You want your friends to be able to tenderly run a knife down the center and for the Romanesco to break apart easily. The salty, tangy, nutty flavor you get from the vinaigrette is the perfect brightness to partner with this earthy veg (which is similar to cauliflower and broccoli). The capers and vinegar make it easy to down a whole head by yourself. . . .

1 large head Romanesco (or broccoli or cauliflower), halved through the core

5 tablespoons extra-virgin olive oil, plus more for drizzling

Kosher salt

3 tablespoons capers, drained

2 teaspoons red wine vinegar

2 teaspoons fresh lemon juice

1 teaspoon honey

1 garlic clove, grated

1 teaspoon finely chopped fresh dill, plus more for serving

⅓ cup pistachios, toasted and roughly chopped

Grated lemon zest, for serving

1 Preheat the oven to 450°F.

2 Bring a large pot of water to a boil. Gently submerge the Romanesco halves in the water (you want them to keep their shape), cover, and boil for 5 minutes. Carefully transfer the Romanesco to a plate or baking sheet lined with paper towels and let it air-dry until the steam has dissipated, about 20 minutes. Don't skimp on this step; a still-steamy and damp Romanesco won't crisp up in the oven.

3 Place the Romanesco on a baking sheet, cut-sides down. Drizzle all over with 2 tablespoons of the olive oil and season WELL with salt. Roast until the cut sides are golden, 15 to 20 minutes. Flip and roast until the Romanesco is golden all over and even a little charred in some places, another 15 to 20 minutes. You'll know it's done when you can easily slide a knife through the middle and it's caramelized and lightly charred in some places. Set aside.

4 In a medium skillet, heat the remaining 3 tablespoons olive oil over medium heat. Add the capers (careful, they might sputter) and cook until they're lightly golden and crispy, about 3 minutes They will open up a bit and look like flowers. Set aside to cool.

5 In a medium bowl, whisk together the vinegar, lemon juice, honey, and garlic. Slowly stream in the capers and oil from the pan as you continue whisking. Season with salt to taste and fold in the dill.

6 Place the Romanesco on a serving plate. Pour the caper vinaigrette over the Romanesco and garnish with dill, the pistachios, and lemon zest.

Whole-Roasted Sweet Potato with Sunflower Gremolata and Lemony Sour Cream

Serves 4

After I had the best whole-roasted sweet potato of my life in Tel Aviv (thank you, Port Said!), I knew I had to write a recipe for this loaded-up bad boy. The secret is to roast the sweet potato at very high heat, so it releases all its delicious sugars that caramelize on the skin. Then to brighten things up, I add sour cream (because what goes better with a roasted potato?) and a sunflower seed and basil gremolata, which adds some much-needed crunch and takes things over the edge into max tastiness.

Roasted Sweet Potatoes

4 sweet potatoes, scrubbed clean

4 tablespoons extra-virgin olive oil

2 teaspoons kosher salt

Sunflower Gremolata

¼ cup sunflower seeds

¼ cup finely sliced fresh basil leaves

¼ cup extra-virgin olive oil

Grated zest of 1 lemon

½ teaspoon kosher salt, plus more to taste

1 garlic clove, grated

Lemony Sour Cream

½ cup sour cream

Juice of ½ lemon (about 1 tablespoon)

¼ teaspoon kosher salt

Serving

Flaky sea salt

Fresh basil leaves, the smallest leaves you can pick

1   **Roast the sweet potatoes:** Preheat the oven to 450°F.

2   Place the sweet potatoes in a baking dish. Rub each potato with 1 tablespoon of the olive oil and ½ teaspoon of the kosher salt. Roast until the skin is crispy and beginning to caramelize, 45 minutes to 1 hour. You want the sugars to start seeping out and caramelizing.

3   **Make the sunflower gremolata:** Toast the sunflower seeds in a dry pan over low heat until fragrant, about 5 minutes, then roughly chop them.

4   In a medium bowl, toss together the sunflower seeds, basil, olive oil, lemon zest, kosher salt, and garlic. Adjust the seasoning with more kosher salt, if desired.

5   **Make the lemony sour cream:** In a small bowl, mix together the sour cream, lemon juice, and kosher salt.

6   **To serve:** Split each sweet potato down the middle and fill each half with 2 tablespoons of the lemony sour cream and 2 tablespoons of the gremolata. Finish with a sprinkle of the sea salt and garnish with the small basil leaves.

NOTE *Go with the smallest sweet potatoes you can find—they're sweeter and easier to cook evenly.*

Roasted Cauliflower with Date-Parsley Gremolata

Serves 4

You could roast a whole head of cauliflower . . . or you could break it up into florets so that you get tons of crispy bits of tender, meaty cauliflower. Its deep, roast-y deliciousness is the perfect counterpoint to the sweet, herbaceous date-parsley gremolata. You are going to be blown away by how much brightness you get from the preserved lemon and how the dates balance the tartness with their dense sweetness.

Roasted Cauliflower

1 large head of cauliflower, cut into florets

2 tablespoons extra-virgin olive oil

1½ teaspoons kosher salt

Gremolata

½ cup chopped pitted Medjool dates (about 5)

½ cup chopped fresh parsley

¼ cup extra-virgin olive oil

1 tablespoon red wine vinegar

1½ tablespoons finely chopped preserved lemon rind, store-bought or homemade (see page 53)

1 garlic clove, minced

1 teaspoon kosher salt

1 **Roast the cauliflower:** Preheat the oven to 500°F.

2 In a large bowl, toss the cauliflower with the olive oil and salt. Spread the mixture on a baking sheet (or two—you want to make sure that the florets have room to breathe so that they get caramelized and crispy instead of steamed) and roast until the cauliflower is golden brown, 20 to 25 minutes.

3 **Make the gremolata:** In a medium bowl, mix together the dates, parsley, olive oil, vinegar, preserved lemon, garlic, and salt. If making this ahead, leave out the vinegar until just before you serve.

4 Scatter the gremolata over the roasted cauliflower and serve.

Whole-Roasted Broccoli with Herbed Yogurt, Dukkah, and Chile

Serves 6

If there were ever a vegetable that deserved a makeover, broccoli is it. When you think of broccoli, you might imagine that bland, over-steamed green mush that your mom made you eat when you were little, and just the thought of it makes you nauseous. Amiright? So we're going to give it a little love, because that's really all broccoli needs—plus super-high heat—to make it truly delicious. When you roast it whole, the little trees get crisp and crunchy at the tips. Topped with cool, creamy yogurt blended with tons of fresh herbs and crunchy, spiced dukkah, it'll be hard to believe that you ever didn't like broccoli.

Roasted Broccoli

2 heads of broccoli

2 tablespoons extra-virgin olive oil

Kosher salt

Herbed Yogurt

1 cup whole-milk Greek yogurt

½ cup chopped fresh parsley

½ cup chopped fresh chives

1 tablespoon chopped fresh tarragon

Juice of ½ lemon

1½ teaspoons kosher salt

1 garlic clove

Serving

Extra-virgin olive oil

Dukkah (page 60)

1 serrano pepper, very thinly sliced

1 lemon

Flaky sea salt

1 Roast the broccoli: Preheat the oven to 425°F. Line a sheet pan with parchment paper.

2 Bring a large pot of water to a boil. Gently lower in the broccoli and boil for 5 minutes. Transfer to a plate or sheet pan lined with paper towels and let the broccoli air-dry.

3 Once the broccoli has stopped steaming, place it on the prepared baking sheet. Drizzle with the olive oil and generously sprinkle with the kosher salt. Roast until golden and lightly charred in some places, 20 to 30 minutes, depending on how hot your oven is.

4 Make the herbed yogurt: In a blender, combine the yogurt, parsley, chives, tarragon, lemon juice, kosher salt, and garlic. Blend until smooth.

5 To serve: Place the roasted broccoli on a serving platter and drizzle over the yogurt and some olive oil. Sprinkle with the dukkah and serrano, add a squeeze of lemon juice and pinch of sea salt, and serve warm.

Winter Squash with Crispy Sage and Honey

Serves 4

I love the caramel-y, pie-like flavor that squash develops as it roasts; adding crispy sage and honey is really just a bonus—and my favorite combo with squash. After you make this, you'll see why. That crispy sweet sage after it roasts? Come on. The fact that you can also eat the skin of most varieties (including my favorite, delicata) is such a win for me—namely because it's that much less prep.

1 kabocha or 2 delicata squash (acorn will work, too, or a mix), cut into ½-inch-thick slices, seeds removed, if desired

15 fresh sage leaves

2 tablespoons extra-virgin olive oil

2 tablespoons honey

2 teaspoons kosher salt

½ teaspoon freshly ground black pepper

1 Preheat the oven to 425°F.

2 On a baking sheet, toss the squash and sage with the olive oil, honey, salt, and pepper. Roast until the squash is tender and golden, 20 to 25 minutes, flipping once about halfway through. Serve.

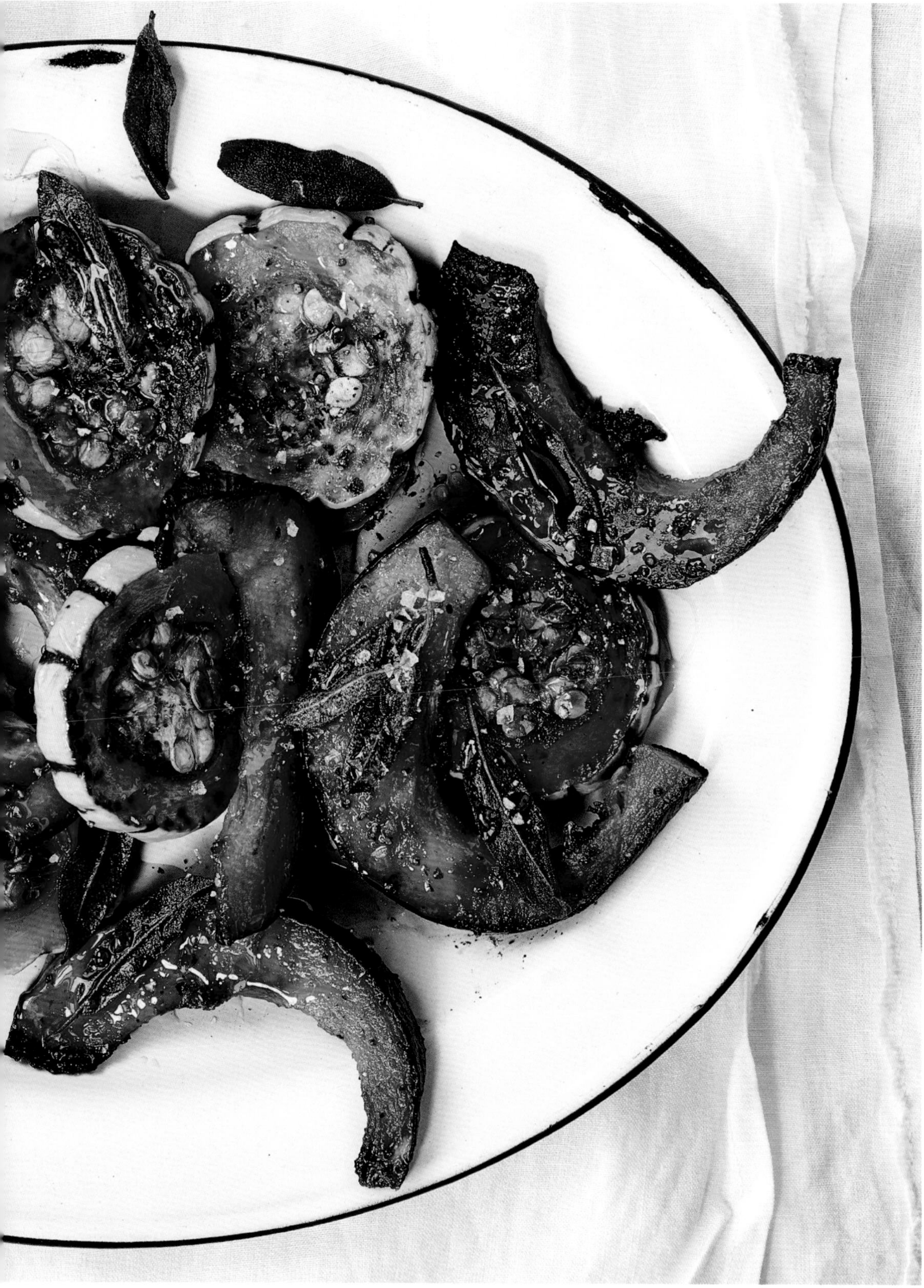

Crispy Smashed Potatoes with Chimichurri and Urfa

Potatoes

Kosher salt

3 pounds new potatoes

¼ cup plus 1 tablespoon extra-virgin olive oil

Freshly ground black pepper

Chimichurri

½ cup roughly chopped fresh dill

½ cup roughly chopped fresh parsley

1 small shallot, finely chopped

1 small or ½ large garlic clove, grated

1½ teaspoons red wine vinegar

1 teaspoon kosher salt

½ teaspoon freshly ground black pepper

½ cup plus 2 tablespoons extra-virgin olive oil

Serving

1½ teaspoons Urfa pepper, cayenne pepper, or chili powder

Chopped fresh parsley

Extra-virgin olive oil

Flaky sea salt

Serves 6

You often see chimichurri paired with meat because of the way its vinegar and herbs brighten and balance. But when you pair it with creamy, starchy potatoes and a sprinkle of smoky Urfa? Forget it. It's an absolute must-make.

1   **Make the potatoes:** Bring a large pot of salted water to a boil. Add the potatoes and cook until tender, about 10 minutes. Drain the potatoes well, shaking off any excess water, and let cool slightly.

2   Preheat the oven to 425°F.

3   Once the potatoes are just cool enough to handle (they'll still be warm), spread them across one or two baking sheets to leave plenty of room between them. With the heel of your hand or the bottom of a glass, gently smash each potato until about ½ inch thick. Drizzle the potatoes with the olive oil, season well with kosher salt and black pepper, and roast until crispy and golden all over, about 25 minutes.

4   **Make the chimichurri:** In a food processor, combine the dill, parsley, shallot, garlic, vinegar, kosher salt, and black pepper. Pulse until the mixture is finely chopped. Continuing to pulse, stream in the olive oil just until the mixture forms a loose sauce.

5   **To serve:** Arrange the roasted potatoes on a platter and generously drizzle with the chimichurri. Sprinkle with the Urfa and parsley, drizzle with olive oil, and finish with a pinch of sea salt.

Garlicky Nigella Green Beans

Serves 4

When green beans are in season in the summer, you don't want to do a whole lot to mess with their crisp sweetness. A quick dip in boiling water takes away any starchiness, and after tossing them with lots of garlic, lemon, and nigella, you have a super-simple, super-quick, and super-fresh plate of veg that's perfect for warm-weather meals. What can I say? It's just super. Other beans would work here, too, like romanos, which I also love.

1½ teaspoons kosher salt, plus more for boiling the water

1 pound green beans (about 3 cups), trimmed

¼ cup extra-virgin olive oil

1 tablespoon nigella seeds or sesame seeds, lightly toasted (or no seeds at all—this will still be insane)

1 large garlic clove, grated

Grated zest of 1 lemon

Juice of ½ lemon

Bring a large pot of salted water to a boil. Add the green beans and cook until just tender, about 1 minute. Drain and transfer the beans immediately to a serving bowl. Toss with the salt, olive oil, nigella seeds, garlic, lemon zest, and lemon juice and serve warm.

Charred Whole Eggplant with Crushed Tomatoes, Basil, and Mint

Serves 6

Almost every restaurant in Israel has a version of this whole-roasted eggplant, so it only made sense to have my own. Serving eggplants whole, stem and all, makes for such a special dish because people can see the vegetable in its beautiful original (or original-ish) form. It's also the perfect blank canvas for a variety of flavors and textures. Sometimes I'm in the mood for a drizzle of pomegranate molasses and yogurt, while other times I add crushed ripe tomato for its bright acidity, balanced with nutty tahini and earthy za'atar. You're going to want a whole loaf of bread or challah for this one.

3 medium eggplants

1 medium tomato

½ teaspoon kosher salt

1 tablespoon za'atar, store-bought or homemade (see page 31)

1½ tablespoons extra-virgin olive oil, plus more for serving

½ cup Garlicky Tahini (page 37)

1 tablespoon Red Zhug (optional; page 50)

⅓ cup fresh basil leaves

⅓ cup fresh mint leaves

Flaky sea salt

Thick slices of sourdough, challah, or pita, for serving

1   With the tip of your knife, pierce each eggplant in two places—it doesn't need to be perfect or in the same place every time; this is just so the eggplant doesn't explode on you.

2   **Pick a cooking method for the eggplant:** grill, broiler, or stovetop burners. The bottom line is that you want this eggplant to be almost unrecognizably charred. It's going to deflate and the skin will get white in some places, but that just means the fire is working its magic on that eggplant.

OPTION 1: Grill Preheat the grill until hot. Add the eggplants and let the fire do its thing, making sure to keep turning the eggplants so they char all over. You want them to get black and maybe even white in some places, 20 to 30 minutes total.

OPTION 2: Broil Preheat the broiler. Put the eggplants in a broilerproof roasting pan and place the pan as close to the heating element as possible. (You may have to adjust your oven rack to accommodate the depth of the pan and eggplants.) Broil until they are evenly charred all over, 35 to 40 minutes, checking and turning the eggplants periodically. You want the eggplants to keep their shape but get really charred and wilted.

OPTION 3: Stovetop Gas Burners Line your stovetop around your burners with foil. Working with one at a time, place the eggplant over a medium flame and let it char, making sure to turn it every 5 minutes. Continue cooking until it is deflated and black all over, about 15 minutes.

(recipe continues)

3 Transfer the cooked eggplants to a colander in the sink and let the juices run. (The juices can make the dish taste bitter.) Once they're cool enough to handle, and being careful to maintain the original shape, remove all of the eggplant skin except for the stem. (Feel free to reserve the skin to make Charred Tahini, page 38.) Set aside on a large platter.

4 In a blender or food processor, blend together the tomato with the kosher salt. Set aside.

5 In a small bowl, mix together the za'atar and olive oil. Set aside.

6 Gently press on the eggplant flesh with a fork to spread it out. Drizzle the eggplants with the garlicky tahini and spoon over the pureed tomato. Drizzle with the za'atar oil and some red zhug (if using). Garnish with the basil and mint and finish with a drizzle of olive oil and a sprinkle of sea salt. Serve warm with fresh bread.

Shawarma-Roasted Carrots with Falafel Crumble and Labneh

Serves 4

I'm a big fan of treating vegetables like meat in the way that you season and cook them. The results are robust, satisfying, and undeniably sexy. In this case, carrots are rubbed with a spice mix usually reserved for shawarma. You could pause there and finish the dish with lemon zest and tons of fresh cilantro, or go the extra mile and add fried falafel bits for texture. Or Option C: Shape the falafel mixture into balls and serve them as you traditionally would with pita, hummus, pickles, and zhug.

Roasted Carrots

2 bunches of carrots (about 12)

2 tablespoons extra-virgin olive oil

2 teaspoons Shawarma Spice Blend (recipe follows) or store-bought

1 teaspoon kosher salt

Falafel

½ cup dried chickpeas, soaked overnight

1 small yellow onion, roughly chopped

3 garlic cloves, peeled

¾ cup fresh parsley, stems and leaves

¾ cup fresh cilantro, stems and leaves

1 teaspoon kosher salt, plus more for sprinkling

1 tablespoon Harissa (page 46)

½ teaspoon ground cardamom

½ teaspoon ground coriander

½ teaspoon baking powder

Grapeseed oil, for frying

Serving

1 cup labneh, store-bought or homemade (page 52)

Grated zest and juice of 1 lemon

Fresh cilantro leaves

1 **Roast the carrots:** Preheat the oven to 450°F.

2 Trim and peel the carrots, then slice them in half lengthwise. On a baking sheet, toss the carrots with the olive oil, shawarma spice blend, and salt. Roast until the edges begin to crisp, 20 to 25 minutes.

3 **Make the falafel:** In a large bowl, combine the chickpeas, 1 teaspoon water, the onion halves, garlic, parsley, cilantro, salt, harissa, cardamom, coriander, and baking powder. Working in one to two batches, add the mixture to a food processor and blitz until you have a fine texture. Combine the batches in a medium bowl and mix.

4 Pour ½ inch grapeseed oil into a deep skillet and heat to 375°F over medium-high heat. To test if the oil is hot enough, drop in a tiny bit of the falafel mixture. It should bubble and float. Press a handful of the falafel mixture between your hands and then sprinkle it into the oil. You want both bigger and smaller chunks. Fry until the outside is golden and crisp, about 1 minute. Remove the falafel from the oil with a slotted spoon, transfer to a plate lined with paper towels, and sprinkle immediately with salt.

5 **To serve:** Spread the labneh in a thick layer on a large plate or platter. Lay the carrots over the labneh and spoon the falafel crumble on top. Finish with the lemon zest and juice and a sprinkling of fresh cilantro.

(recipe continues)

SHAWARMA SPICE BLEND

Makes about ¼ cup

Shawarma spice mix can be difficult to find at the store, and I don't want that to stand in your way of making the dishes that call for it or using it as a dry rub for meats or dusting it over veggies before they roast. It has an earthy-sweet flavor profile with a little bit of heat (because I love adding cayenne), but if you don't have every single one of these spices, that's fine, too—everyone has their own version of shawarma, and that'll just be yours.

1 tablespoon ground cumin

1 tablespoon ground coriander

1 teaspoon ground allspice

1 teaspoon sweet paprika

1 teaspoon ground turmeric

1 teaspoon freshly ground black pepper

½ teaspoon cayenne pepper

½ teaspoon ground cardamom

½ teaspoon ground cinnamon

In a medium bowl, combine the cumin, coriander, allspice, paprika, turmeric, black pepper, cayenne pepper, cardamom, and cinnamon. Mix thoroughly. The spice blend can last up to 6 months in an airtight container.

Harissa-Roasted Tomato and Chickpea Soup with Lime Yogurt

Serves 8

I've always loved roasted tomato soup, and that's pretty much what this is. You're tossing the tomatoes in spices and harissa, then letting the oven do all the work of getting them caramelized and slightly charred. After that, there's not much more to it than pureeing them, tossing in chickpeas (from a can!), and simmering the mixture on the stove so the flavors can reduce and intensify even more. Finally, it all gets topped with a tart and tangy lime yogurt that brightens the deep roasted flavors.

Soup

10 medium tomatoes

2 large yellow onions

10 garlic cloves—
9 unpeeled, 1 minced

⅔ cup plus 1 tablespoon extra-virgin olive oil

⅓ cup harissa, store-bought or homemade (see page 46)

3 teaspoons kosher salt

2 teaspoons ground coriander

1½ teaspoons ground cumin

1¼ teaspoons ground turmeric

½ teaspoon smoked paprika

½ teaspoon freshly ground black pepper

2 (15.5-ounce) cans chickpeas, rinsed and drained

1 tablespoon grated fresh ginger

½ fresh cayenne chile or Thai red chile (optional)

3 cups vegetable stock or water

Lime Yogurt

1 cup whole-milk Greek yogurt

Grated zest and juice of 1 lime

½ teaspoon kosher salt

Serving

Kosher salt and freshly ground black pepper

Harissa, store-bought or homemade (see page 46)

Chopped fresh mint

1 **Make the soup:** Preheat the oven to 450°F.

2 Roughly chop the tomatoes and onions. In a large bowl, combine the tomatoes, onions, whole garlic cloves, ⅔ cup of the olive oil, the harissa, 2 teaspoons of the salt, the coriander, 1 teaspoon of the cumin, 1 teaspoon of the turmeric, the smoked paprika, and the black pepper. Spread the mixture on a baking sheet and roast until golden and lightly charred, about 30 minutes. Peel the roasted garlic cloves. Carefully transfer the mixture to a blender and blend until smooth.

3 In a large pot, heat the remaining 1 tablespoon olive oil over medium-high heat. Add the chickpeas, ginger, minced garlic, chile (if using), and the remaining 1 teaspoon salt, ½ teaspoon cumin, and ¼ teaspoon turmeric. Sauté until the chickpeas begin to soften slightly, about 5 minutes. Add the blended roasted tomato mixture and the vegetable stock. Bring to a boil, reduce the heat to a simmer, and cook for 45 minutes to thicken the soup.

4 **Make the lime yogurt:** In a medium bowl, whisk together the yogurt, lime zest, lime juice, and salt.

5 **To serve:** Taste the soup to check for seasoning and adjust if needed. Serve in bowls with a dollop of the lime yogurt and a swirl of harissa. Garnish with fresh mint.

Meat and Fish,
So Delish

I promise you that the recipes in this chapter will get it done every time.

When I started thinking about what dishes to include in this book, I knew I wanted to celebrate all the big, bold flavors that I've loved so much since I was a little girl. But I also knew—especially as a mom to a young kid—that these dishes couldn't just be for show; they had to actually deliver, in flavor and in simplicity. When it comes to getting dinner on the table, these recipes will impress *and* are easy enough for weeknights, including all the big, meaty (and fishy) dishes that tend to be a little intimidating.

Meat and Fish, So Delish

Braised Halibut with Roasted Cherry Tomatoes and Tahini (Chraime)

Serves 6

This North African dish, known as *chraime* (pronounced *chr-eye-may*—really let your back-of-the-throat *cchhh* rip) is inspired by a simple but rich dish traditionally made by the Sephardic Jews. For this version, we're making a flavorful base with juicy ripe tomatoes, peppers, and spices for braising flaky halibut, and I fancied it up by adding some dry white wine for brightness. One tip: Be sure your sauce is seasoned properly because that's what is giving your fish its flavor.

2 bunches cherry tomatoes on the vine, or 2 cups cherry tomatoes

5 tablespoons extra-virgin olive oil, plus more for serving

Kosher salt and freshly ground black pepper

1 large yellow onion, finely diced

1 red bell pepper, finely diced

3 garlic cloves, minced

1 tablespoon harissa, store-bought or homemade (see page 46)

1 teaspoon sweet paprika

½ teaspoon ground turmeric

¼ teaspoon smoked paprika

⅓ cup dry white wine

6 medium tomatoes, chopped

6 halibut fillets (4 to 5 ounces each) or other white, flaky fish such as striped bass, sea bass, or cod, skinned

Garlicky Tahini (page 37)

Chopped fresh herbs, such as basil and dill, for garnish

1 Preheat the oven to 425°F. Place the cherry tomatoes on a baking sheet and drizzle with 2 tablespoons of the olive oil. Season well with salt and roast until charred and bursting, about 15 minutes.

2 In a large, deep skillet, heat the remaining 3 tablespoons olive oil over medium heat. Add the onion and bell pepper and season with salt and pepper to taste. Cook until the onion is translucent, about 5 minutes. Add the garlic, harissa, sweet paprika, turmeric, and smoked paprika and cook for 1 minute. Add the white wine and use your spoon to scrape up the browned bits from the bottom of the pan. Let the mixture simmer for 2 more minutes, then reduce heat to medium-low. Add the chopped tomatoes, season with salt and pepper, and cover. Cook, stirring occasionally, until the tomatoes begin to break down and start to resemble a sauce, 10 to 15 minutes. Remove the lid and cook until slightly reduced, another 10 minutes.

3 Check the sauce for seasoning and increase the heat to a simmer. Let it reduce until it's thickened slightly, about 5 minutes, which will make it more flavorful and help it cling to the fish. Place the halibut in the pan, making sure to spoon sauce over the fish. Cover and simmer until the fish is no longer translucent in the middle and the flesh is flaky, 6 to 8 minutes.

4 Serve right in the pan with the garlicky tahini drizzled over it and topped with the roasted cherry tomatoes, fresh herbs, and additional olive oil.

Chermoula
Sea Bass

Serves 8

Chermoula is a North African marinade-relish hybrid that's packed with herbs and aromatics. I particularly love steaming fish that's been bathed in chermoula, letting all those bold flavors seep in. Finish it with a squeeze of lemon to brighten everything up, and you're done.

8 Mediterranean sea bass fillets (6 ounces each), skinned (see Note)

Kosher salt and freshly ground black pepper

3 tablespoons Chermoula (page 45)

Chopped fresh parsley, for serving

2 lemons, cut into wedges, for serving

NOTE *You can use a number of different types of fish here. I prefer whitefish like sea bass, striped bass, and branzino, but this would also be amazing with salmon or swordfish.*

1 Preheat the oven to 425°F.

2 Season the fish on both sides with salt and pepper and rub all over with the chermoula. Place each fillet on a piece of parchment paper and fold it into a tightly sealed packet. Place them on a baking sheet and roast for 10 minutes. Serve immediately with the parsley and lemon wedges.

Seared Scallops with Basil-Turmeric Butter

Serves 2 to 4

I've heard people complain about cooking scallops at home because of the smell, but I say Eff that! Turn on your vent! If it's delicious, a little extra aroma shouldn't matter. And these scallops *deliver* with minimal effort. All you have to do is get a great sear on them, baste them with butter, and serve them doused in fresh lemon juice. I do call for the butter to be a compound butter—softened butter that's been laced with basil and turmeric—which, granted, is one extra step. But it will take you *maybe* 5 extra minutes and adds so much dimension and depth of flavor to the scallops.

1 pound sea scallops

Kosher salt and freshly ground black pepper

2 tablespoons extra-virgin olive oil

2 tablespoons Basil-Turmeric Butter (recipe follows)

Juice of 1 lemon

1 Pat the scallops dry with paper towels and season well with salt and pepper. In a large skillet, heat the oil over medium-high heat. Add the scallops and sear—ideally without moving them—until deeply golden on both sides, about 2 minutes per side. Reduce the heat and add the basil-turmeric butter to the pan, spooning it over the scallops as it melts, about 30 seconds. Transfer the scallops to a platter.

2 Squeeze a ton of lemon juice over the top and serve immediately.

BASIL-TURMERIC BUTTER

Makes about ½ cup

Use this butter to dress any seafood, chicken, or just toast.

½ cup finely chopped fresh basil

¼ cup chopped fresh parsley

8 tablespoons (1 stick) unsalted butter, at room temperature

Grated zest of 1 lemon

1 teaspoon ground coriander

½ teaspoon ground turmeric

½ garlic clove, grated

Kosher salt and freshly ground black pepper

In a medium bowl, combine the basil, parsley, butter, lemon zest, coriander, turmeric, garlic, and salt and pepper to taste. Mix thoroughly so all of the herbs and spices are really incorporated into the butter. Taste and adjust for seasoning. Store in the fridge for up to 1 week.

Whole-Roasted Branzino with Harissa, Garlic, and Lemon

Serves 4

Branzino is one of my favorite fish to roast whole. It's flaky and sweet and doesn't need much to make it delicious, but this garlic harissa sauce would be amazing slathered on any fish, such as wild salmon or swordfish. The oils seep in to the white flesh of the fish, making it spicy, garlicky, and beautifully ruby red. I highly recommend serving this over an aromatic bed of grains, like the Date and Dill Rice (page 232), and alongside a fresh salad.

3 tablespoons harissa, store-bought or homemade (see page 46)

3 garlic cloves, peeled and left whole

1 small shallot, roughly chopped

1 teaspoon honey

½ teaspoon ground cumin

3 teaspoons kosher salt

2 tablespoons extra-virgin olive oil, plus more for drizzling

2 whole branzino, cleaned (let your fishmonger do this for you)

Freshly ground black pepper

2 lemons, sliced

Date and Dill Rice (page 232) or other cooked grains, for serving

1 Preheat the oven to 425°F.

2 In a blender or using a mortar and pestle, combine the harissa, garlic, shallot, honey, cumin, and 1 teaspoon of the salt. Blend until combined. Add the olive oil and pulse until just combined. (Don't overdo it or the oil will get bitter—that's why I like the mortar and pestle. If using a mortar and pestle, smush and mix until evenly combined.)

3 Carefully use a sharp knife to score each side of the fish, making 5 or 6 incisions into the skin and flesh of the fish (this will help even more flavor seep in to the flesh). Place the fish on a baking sheet and season with the remaining 2 teaspoons salt and pepper to taste. Rub them all over, inside and out, with the garlic-harissa sauce.

4 Stuff each fish with lemons and place the remaining slices under the fish. Roast until the flesh of the fish is firm and white, 20 to 25 minutes. Drizzle with a little more olive oil.

5 Serve with the date and dill rice or any other piping-hot plate of grains.

Sumac-Roasted Snapper with Lime Yogurt

Serves 4

I've been obsessed with Persian cuisine for most of my adult life, reading tons of books on the topic and, obviously, eating all the food there is to eat. One combination that comes up again and again is sumac, lime, and yogurt. This whole roasted fish recipe is the perfect place to put that trinity to work. When you smother the fish in sumac—literally packing it into the skin like you're giving it a clay mask—it forms a crisp crust while infusing the fish with its unique floral acidity.

Roasted Snapper

1 whole red snapper, cleaned

2 tablespoons sumac

2 teaspoons kosher salt

¼ teaspoon freshly ground black pepper

2 garlic cloves, thinly sliced

2 tablespoons extra-virgin olive oil

Lime Yogurt

1 cup whole-milk Greek yogurt

Grated zest and juice of 1 lime

½ teaspoon kosher salt

1 garlic clove, grated

Serving

Chopped fresh mint

Juice of 1 lime

2 limes, cut into wedges

1 **Roast the snapper:** Preheat the oven to 425°F.

2 Carefully use a sharp knife to score each side of the fish, making 5 or 6 incisions into the skin and flesh of the fish (this will help even more flavor seep in to the flesh). Season inside and out with the sumac, salt, and pepper. Really pack on the sumac! Place the fish on a baking sheet. Stuff with the sliced garlic and drizzle the olive oil all over. Roast until the eyes have popped and the flesh is firm to the touch, about 20 minutes.

3 **Make the lime yogurt:** In a medium bowl, stir together the yogurt, lime zest, lime juice, salt, and grated garlic.

4 **To serve:** Place the roasted fish on a serving platter and scatter mint over the top. Squeeze the lime juice over the fish and serve the yogurt and lime wedges on the side.

My Brisket

Show me a Jewish home, and I'll show you a brisket recipe—almost every Eastern European Jewish family has its own version. While I love my mom's, I wanted to honor the fact that it's now my turn to get my matriarch on and develop one of my own. This recipe pays homage to the traditional flavor, but gives the whole thing a little facelift. One key update is taking it out of the oven halfway through cooking to slice it, then returning it to the sauce to finish braising. The sauce bastes every nook and cranny, and you have an insurance policy against your tender AF brisket becoming a hot mess when you try to slice it after the fact. No need to wait for a special holiday to make this guy— Lemony Yogurt (page 56) and a nice fresh salad make it a meal perfect for any get-together.

1 brisket (5 pounds)

Kosher salt and freshly ground black pepper

3 tablespoons extra-virgin olive oil

4 large carrots, cut into 1-inch rounds

1 large yellow onion, finely chopped

2 celery stalks, finely chopped

3 garlic cloves, finely chopped

1 tablespoon grated fresh ginger

2 tablespoons tomato paste

1 tablespoon coriander seeds

1 teaspoon ground cumin

2 cups dry white wine

4 cups beef stock

1 tablespoon minced preserved lemon rind, store-bought or homemade (see page 53)

Lemony Yogurt (page 56), for serving

1 Preheat the oven to 350°F.

2 Season the brisket liberally on both sides with salt and pepper. In a large Dutch oven, heat the oil over medium-high heat. Sear the brisket on both sides until golden, about 5 minutes per side. Transfer the brisket to a large plate and set aside.

3 To the same pot, add the carrots, onion, and celery and season with salt and pepper. Cook over medium heat until the vegetables have softened a bit, 3 to 5 minutes. Add the garlic and ginger and cook for another minute or so, until fragrant. Stir in the tomato paste, coriander, and cumin and cook for another minute. Deglaze with the white wine, stirring and letting the wine cook off a little, about 2 minutes.

4 Return the brisket to the pot and pour in enough beef stock to cover. If the 4 cups of stock doesn't do it, add water until you get there. Increase the heat to medium-high and bring the stock to a boil. Cover the pot, transfer to the oven, and braise for 1 hour 30 minutes.

5 Carefully remove the brisket from the broth and slice it against the grain into ½-inch-thick slices. Stir the preserved lemon into the braising liquid, then return the brisket to the pot, doing your best to keep its original shape. Cover the pot and return to the oven until the brisket is very tender, another 1 hour to 1 hour 30 minutes. Serve warm with the lemony yogurt.

Mom's
Chicken Soup

Serves 4 for a week

This is hands down the most classic Jewish comfort food. My earliest childhood memories involve standing over a pot of chicken soup that my mom would be stirring and skimming. No matter what our ailment was, the offer was always, "Chicken soup?" It's also Ido's favorite meal of all time. If I have a big pot of this on the stove, Ido literally jumps for joy in the kitchen. And I get it—it's the most nourishing food for the soul there is. So of course I had to put a version of it in the book, and it doesn't get more perfect than Mom's. She always stuck to the classics—parsnips, carrots, celery, onion—but I wanted to turn things up a *little*. I've added an entire head of garlic and some turmeric for more depth and even more healing oomph. Plus the turmeric amplifies the broth's golden hue that's always the sign of a solid chicken soup.

1 whole chicken (4 pounds)

3 large carrots, cut into 1-inch chunks

3 celery stalks, cut into 1-inch chunks

2 medium parsnips, peeled and cut into 1-inch chunks

1 large yellow onion, peeled and halved

1 head of garlic, halved horizontally

1 teaspoon ground turmeric

Kosher salt and freshly ground black pepper

1 bunch of parsley, leaves and stems

1 bunch of dill, leaves and stems, plus more leaves for garnish

1 In a large pot, bring 16 to 18 cups of water (enough to cover the chicken) to a boil over medium-high heat. Add the chicken and return to a boil, skimming off any foam or bits that float to the top. Add the carrots, celery, parsnips, onion, garlic, and turmeric. Season well with salt and pepper. Reduce the heat to medium and simmer uncovered for 1 hour, stirring occasionally, until the chicken is cooked through, the vegetables are tender, and the broth is infused with flavor.

2 Stir in the parsley and dill and check again for seasoning. Remove the pot from the heat and let the soup steep, off the heat, for 20 minutes.

3 Remove the chicken and let it cool slightly. Pick the meat off the chicken carcass and tear into bite-size pieces (or use two forks to shred it). Discard the skin and bones along with the herbs. Return the chicken meat to the broth and serve warm, or let the soup cool completely before dividing it among storage containers and storing in the fridge for up to 1 week (it's even better the next day) or in the freezer for up to 1 month.

RANDOM SUGGESTION *Ask your butcher for extra chicken bones, which you can drop into the simmering broth with your chicken as it simmers. The same goes for any chicken carcasses you've saved from making roast chicken.*

Clams with Saffron and Celery

Serves 2

Most of the flavors that come out of Israel are a mix of Mediterranean and Middle Eastern influences, so including a fresh seafood dish that highlights subtle, floral saffron feels like an appropriate nod to that. Plus, I love clams, Ido *loves* clams (and mussels, which you could also use here), and we are all in agreement that any dish you can eat with your hands is pretty hot—right? I'm always surprised that more people aren't cooking clams or mussels, because they're the ultimate no-fail 20-minute meal. You just need to let the wine and aromatics do their thing (including celery, which is completely underrated and a great alternative to fennel, which has already had its moment in this book), grab some bread for sopping up all the briny sauciness in the pan, and you're set.

2 pounds fresh littleneck clams or mussels

5 tablespoons unsalted butter

2 tablespoons extra-virgin olive oil

2 celery stalks (reserve the celery leaves for garnish), finely chopped

1 medium shallot, finely chopped

4 garlic cloves, thinly sliced

Large pinch of saffron threads

Kosher salt and freshly ground black pepper

¾ cup dry white wine

2 tablespoons finely chopped fresh parsley, for serving

Thick slices of sourdough bread or a baguette, for serving

1 In a large bowl, cover the clams or mussels with plenty of cold water and soak for 20 minutes; then drain. Give any open shells a quick tap on the counter and toss any that don't close back up when tapped.

2 In a large pot, heat the butter and olive oil over medium heat. Add the celery, shallot, garlic, and saffron and season with salt and pepper. Cook until the shallot is translucent, about 5 minutes. Increase the heat to high, add the wine and the clams or mussels, cover, and steam until they open up, about 5 minutes. Discard any that don't open. Add the parsley and toss gently. Garnish with the celery leaves and serve immediately with bread.

Baharat Whole-Roasted Chicken with Roasted Shallots, Preserved Lemon, and Sweet Potatoes

Serves 4

Baharat is one of those spice blends where after you've used it once, you start sprinkling it on everything you cook just to see how it transforms a dish. On chicken, it's just magic: The spice blend forms a sort of crispy shell on the skin, and its warm, smoky notes complement the flavor of the meat without overpowering it. My other secret to perfect roast chicken is to slather olive oil underneath the skin over the breast, which keeps the meat really moist. I set the whole thing over sweet potatoes, garlic, and shallots, which act as a roasting rack while bathing in all those unbelievable juices. Serving the chicken and veg with preserved lemon gives everything a bright pop, making this dish decadently addictive.

1 whole chicken
(3 to 4 pounds)

¾ cup extra-virgin olive oil

1½ tablespoons baharat
spice blend, store-bought
or homemade (see
page 22)

Kosher salt and freshly
ground black pepper

2 medium sweet potatoes,
scrubbed clean, cut
lengthwise into 1-inch
wedges

6 shallots, halved lengthwise

1 head of garlic, separated
into cloves, unpeeled

1 preserved lemon
rind, store-bought or
homemade (see page 53),
rinsed and finely chopped

1 Preheat the oven to 425°F.

2 Slide your fingers beneath the skin of the chicken to gently separate it from the meat. Pour ¼ cup of the olive oil over the chicken, rubbing it under the skin and all over the outside of the bird. Season with the baharat, 2 teaspoons salt, and ½ teaspoon pepper (really make sure to cover every bit of the chicken).

3 In a roasting pan, toss the sweet potatoes, shallots, and garlic with another ¼ cup olive oil. Season with salt and pepper and toss again. Set the chicken breast-side up on top of the vegetables. Roast until the chicken is crisp and golden, the juices run clear when it's pierced, and a meat thermometer inserted in a thigh reads 165°F, about 1 hour. Carefully remove the chicken from the pan and tent it with foil. Let it rest while you finish the vegetables.

4 Return the pan with the vegetables to the oven and roast for another 5 minutes. Peel the garlic and discard the skins. Return the roasted cloves to the pan.

5 In a small bowl, mix together the chopped lemon rind and the remaining ¼ cup of olive oil. (If you want to make this a creamier condiment, you could also blend it in a blender.)

6 Carve the chicken (using a very sharp knife) and arrange the pieces on a serving platter. Or, if you're too nervous to carve, just place the chicken on a platter and bring it out for your guests to have at it. Serve the chicken surrounded with the roasted vegetables and drizzled with the preserved lemon oil.

Hubby's Saucy
Spiced Meatballs

Meatballs

4 pita or slices of white
    bread, crusts removed

1 cup whole milk

1 pound ground beef
    (85% lean)

1 small yellow onion,
    finely chopped

¾ cup finely chopped fresh parsley

2 garlic cloves, finely chopped

1 large egg, lightly beaten

1 tablespoon sweet paprika

1 teaspoon smoked paprika

1 teaspoon curry powder

1 teaspoon kosher salt, plus more to taste

½ teaspoon freshly ground black pepper

½ teaspoon ground cumin

Extra-virgin olive oil, for frying

Sauce

3 tablespoons extra-virgin olive oil

3 small yellow onions, finely chopped

3 red bell peppers, finely chopped

Kosher salt and freshly ground black pepper

5 garlic cloves, minced

2 teaspoons Aleppo pepper or red chile flakes

1 tablespoon sweet paprika

1 teaspoon smoked paprika

1 teaspoon curry powder

½ teaspoon ground cumin

2 (14.5-ounce) cans crushed tomatoes (I love San Marzanos)

2 (15.5-ounce) cans chickpeas, rinsed and drained

Leaves from 2 bunches of cilantro, chopped

1 lemon, thinly sliced

¼ cup tomato paste

1 teaspoon sugar

Pinch of ground cinnamon

Serving

Cooked basmati rice (optional)

Serves 6 to 8

When I first met Ido, there were two dishes that he would always brag about making really well. One was chili and the other was these crazy meatballs. I thought (a) you're such a man with your meat- and sauce-based everything, and (b) I love you so much for contributing these dishes to our family (*awwwww*). Seriously, these meatballs are such a revelation, especially the beautiful bright combination of tomatoes, lemon, and chickpeas. And I've never seen anyone use a milk-soaked pita in place of the traditional milk-soaked bread. Genius. This recipe makes a lot of meatballs, so it is a cook-it-on-Sunday, eat-it-through-the-week kinda meal, one that I love pairing with a big pot of rice.

1 Make the meatballs: In a medium bowl, soak the bread in the milk for 2 minutes. Squeeze the bread between your hands until you've removed as much moisture as possible. Discard the milk.

2 In a large bowl, combine the soaked bread, beef, onion, parsley, garlic, egg, sweet paprika, smoked paprika, curry powder, salt, black pepper, and cumin. Mix gently with your hands until combined (the pita will break up and blend as you go). Measure out the mixture in ½-cup portions and roll into balls. Sprinkle with salt.

3 In a heavy-bottomed pot, heat a few tablespoons of olive oil (enough to coat the bottom of the pot) over medium-high heat. Working in batches, sear the meatballs all over until golden, about 5 minutes. Set aside.

4 Make the sauce: Add the oil to the same pot over medium-high heat. Add the onions and bell peppers and season with salt and black pepper. Cook until the onions are translucent, about 5 minutes. Stir in the garlic, Aleppo pepper, sweet paprika, smoked paprika, curry powder, and cumin. Reduce the heat to medium, cover, and cook until the vegetables are soft and the spices are fragrant, about 3 minutes. Stir in 2 cups water, the tomatoes, chickpeas, cilantro, lemon, tomato paste, sugar, and cinnamon. Bring the sauce to a simmer and cook for 10 to 15 minutes, until the tomatoes have broken down and the sauce has thickened slightly. Check the seasoning, adding more salt if desired.

5 Place the seared meatballs in the sauce. Increase the heat to high and bring to a boil. Reduce the heat and simmer, uncovered, until the sauce has thickened and the flavors have intensified, 35 to 40 minutes.

6 To serve: Serve as is or with fluffy basmati rice.

Sticky Lamb Tagine with Apricots, Fennel, and Honey

Serves 6

I have such a crazy obsession with Moroccan food. I love the heady, aromatic ingredients, and especially the tagines. In the simplest terms, tagines are magic. They're essentially either meat or vegetables braised for a long time in beautiful spices and aromatics, dotted with subtly sweet gems and briny, bright bites like dried apricots, prunes, preserved lemons, and olives. For this version, we're going with lamb because it's super classic and the way it's served right off the shank is so indulgently primal. By the end of its staycation in the oven, it should be so tender that you could serve it with a spoon. If you can't, put that baby back into the oven until it submits.

4 lamb shanks

Kosher salt and freshly ground black pepper

1 tablespoon extra-virgin olive oil

3 medium carrots, finely diced

1 large yellow onion, finely diced

1 large fennel bulb, finely diced

2 tablespoons tomato paste

1 tablespoon harissa, store-bought or homemade (see page 46)

3 garlic cloves, minced

1 tablespoon grated fresh ginger

1 teaspoon ground coriander

1 teaspoon cumin seeds

½ teaspoon ground turmeric

Large pinch of good-quality saffron threads

Pinch of ground cinnamon

4 cups chicken stock or water

1 tablespoon honey

¾ cup whole dried apricots

1½ tablespoons chopped preserved lemon rind, store-bought or homemade (see page 53)

Chopped fresh cilantro, for garnish

Brown Butter Couscous (page 226) or other couscous, for serving

1 Preheat the oven to 350°F.

2 Season the lamb liberally with salt and pepper. In a large Dutch oven or other heavy ovenproof pot, heat the oil over medium-high heat. Add the lamb shanks and sear until golden all over, about 10 minutes. Transfer the shanks to a plate and set aside; don't turn off the heat.

3 Add the carrots, onion, and fennel to the pot and season with salt and pepper. Cook just until the vegetables begin to soften, about 6 minutes. Stir in the tomato paste, harissa, garlic, ginger, coriander, cumin seeds, turmeric, saffron, and cinnamon and cook for a minute or two, until the spices are very fragrant. Return the lamb to the pot and add the stock and honey. Increase the heat to high and bring to a boil. Cover and transfer to the oven to cook for 2 hours 30 minutes.

4 Remove the pot from the oven and stir in the apricots and preserved lemon. Replace the lid and return the pot to the oven for another 30 minutes. You want the lamb to be falling off the bone. Top with cilantro and serve hot, with fluffy couscous.

Baked Lamb Kebabs with Roasted Vegetables and Tahini (Siniya)

Serves 4

Siniya (sin-ee-ya) is just so cool. It's a Palestinian dish where the tahini is baked along with the meat (usually ground lamb, though you could use beef or turkey), which creates a whole new texture for my favorite condiment and ensures that every bite gets that garlicky, nutty flavor. Best yet, the brilliant way all the simple steps of the recipe come together in one baking dish makes this a win for me.

Vegetables

2 large sweet potatoes, scrubbed clean, cut into 1-inch-thick rounds

½ head of cauliflower, florets roughly separated

1½ cups cherry tomatoes

1 large red onion, roughly chopped

1 head of garlic, separated into cloves, unpeeled

⅓ cup extra-virgin olive oil

2 teaspoons kosher salt

¼ teaspoon freshly ground black pepper

Lamb Kebabs

1 pound ground lamb (or beef or turkey)

1 cup chopped fresh parsley

¼ cup pine nuts, toasted in a dry pan until fragrant

1 large shallot, finely diced

2 garlic cloves, grated

1 teaspoon kosher salt

½ teaspoon ground coriander

½ teaspoon ground cumin

¼ teaspoon freshly ground black pepper

Pinch of ground cinnamon

Finishing and Serving

1 cup Garlicky Tahini (page 37)

Kosher salt and freshly ground black pepper

Green Zhug (page 50)

1 Prepare the vegetables: Preheat the oven to 450°F.

2 In an 11 x 15-inch baking dish (large enough to spread the vegetables out in a single layer so they brown, not steam), combine the sweet potatoes, cauliflower, tomatoes, onion, garlic, olive oil, salt, and pepper. Toss thoroughly to coat. Roast until the vegetables are lightly charred, about 25 minutes.

3 Meanwhile, make the lamb kebabs: In a large bowl, combine the lamb, parsley, pine nuts, shallot, garlic, salt, coriander, cumin, pepper, and cinnamon. Mix gently with your hands to combine. Form the mixture into 8 small patties.

4 To finish and serve: In a small bowl, whisk together the garlicky tahini and 3 tablespoons water to thin it out slightly.

5 When the vegetables are lightly charred, place the patties directly on top and sprinkle with salt and pepper on both sides. Drizzle everything with the thinned garlicky tahini and return to the oven until the lamb is cooked to medium, 10 to 12 minutes. Serve with green zhug over the top or on the side.

Chermoula Pork Chops with Labneh and Charred Shallots

Serves 4

This dish is my way of reminding myself that pork is out there in the world and I don't eat enough of it. It's more of a quick whip-up than other meaty cuts like lamb leg, and it's not as big of a commitment in terms of increasing when needing to feed 6-plus people. Plus it's such a great, fatty (if you're doing it right) canvas for just about any flavors, but especially this herbaceous chermoula.

6 large shallots, halved lengthwise

3 tablespoons extra-virgin olive oil

Kosher salt and freshly ground black pepper

4 bone-in pork chops, about 1 inch thick

¼ cup Chermoula (page 45)

Chopped fresh cilantro, for serving

Labneh, store-bought or homemade (page 52), for serving

1   Preheat the oven to 350°F.

2   On a baking sheet, toss together the shallots, 1 tablespoon of the olive oil, and a sprinkle of salt and pepper. Roast, tossing occasionally, until the shallots are jammy and fragrant, about 30 minutes. Remove from the oven but leave the oven on and increase the temperature to 450°F.

3   Generously season both sides of the pork chops with salt and pepper. Preheat a large ovenproof skillet or grill pan with the remaining 2 tablespoons olive oil over medium-high heat. Cook the pork chops until they are nicely charred on the outside but still juicy on the inside, 3 to 4 minutes per side. Finish in the oven for another 5 minutes.

4   Top each pork chop with a schmear of chermoula and a sprinkle of cilantro. Serve with the charred shallots and labneh.

Stuffed Tomatoes with Beef, Eggplant, and Currants

Serves 8

Jewish people love stuffing vegetables—peppers, zucchini, cabbage—something that most of us get from our Eastern European roots. I wanted to honor that with a pretty traditional filling found in Middle Eastern cuisine (rice, beef, cumin, currants) but chose beautiful ripe tomatoes as the vessel, which is a little more bistro than babushka. The tomatoes melt as they bake, infusing the filling with their juices, and the whole deal gets topped off with crunchy, garlicky bread crumbs.

Stuffed Tomatoes

1 small eggplant, sliced crosswise into ¼-inch-thick slices

4 tablespoons extra-virgin olive oil

Kosher salt

16 medium tomatoes

½ cup basmati rice

1 small yellow onion, chopped

2 garlic cloves, minced

¼ teaspoon ground turmeric

¼ teaspoon ground coriander

¼ teaspoon ground cumin

Small pinch of ground cinnamon

1½ tablespoons harissa, store-bought or homemade (see page 46)

1 tablespoon tomato paste

½ pound ground beef (85% lean)

¼ cup currants or other chopped dried fruit such as raisins, dates, or apricots

Garlicky Bread Crumbs

1 cup panko bread crumbs

2 tablespoons extra-virgin olive oil, plus more for drizzling

1 garlic clove, grated

¼ teaspoon kosher salt

1 **Make the stuffed tomatoes:** Preheat the oven to 350°F.

2 In a medium bowl, toss the eggplant with 2 tablespoons of the olive oil and a sprinkle of salt. Arrange the eggplant slices on a baking sheet and roast until golden brown, 10 to 15 minutes. Flip the slices and repeat. Set aside.

3 Thinly slice off the tops of the tomatoes and use a spoon to gently scoop the pulp out into a bowl. Be sure to leave a sturdy shell to stuff the filling into. Place the gutted tomatoes on a sheet pan and set aside. Roughly chop the tomato pulp and set aside.

4 In a sieve, rinse the rice for 1 minute under cool running water. Bring a large pot of salted water to a boil, add the rice, and cook the rice for half of the time recommended on the package. (The rice will continue to cook in the tomato, so you're just parcooking it here.) Drain the rice and return it to the empty pot. Dice the roasted eggplant and add it to the rice. Set aside.

5 In a large skillet, heat the remaining 2 tablespoons oil over medium-high heat. Add the onion, garlic, turmeric, coriander, cumin, cinnamon, and harissa and cook until the onion is translucent, about 5 minutes. Stir in the reserved tomato pulp and the tomato paste and cook until reduced slightly, about another 3 minutes. Add the beef and continue cooking until the beef has browned, 7 to 10 minutes. Remove the pan from the heat and add the currants and the rice-eggplant mixture. Mix thoroughly to combine and season well with more salt, if needed.

6 Fill the hollowed-out tomatoes with the beef and rice mixture and set them back on the sheet.

7 **Make the garlicky bread crumbs:** In a blender or food processor, pulse the bread crumbs until fine. Add the olive oil, garlic, and salt. Pulse briefly to combine.

8 Top the stuffed tomatoes with the bread crumbs and drizzle about a teaspoon of olive oil over each tomato. Bake for about 30 minutes, or until the bread crumbs are golden brown and crisp and the rice is cooked through.

Big Bowls
of Grains

A big pot of grains is an opportunity to play.

(And we're including couscous here because, let's be honest, though it's technically a mini pasta, it's an honorary member of the tribe). It's the perfect vehicle for mixing textures and flavors, including tons of fresh herbs, nuts and seeds, dried or fresh fruit, and, of course, spices. A beautiful platter of steaming, fluffy grains is a meal in and of itself, but it's also right up there with bread as an essential meal accompaniment. Grains are perfect for sopping up sauces, while adding even more interesting notes to your main dish.

I love making big batches of grain salads to keep in the fridge and eat throughout the week. I always envisioned myself as this woman who would consistently have her fridge stocked with fresh salads to go along with her homemade pickles and sauces . . . and I get there about 5 percent of the time (the rest of it, I'm just running around like a headless chicken). But when I do, the grain salads in this chapter are what I'm reaching for.

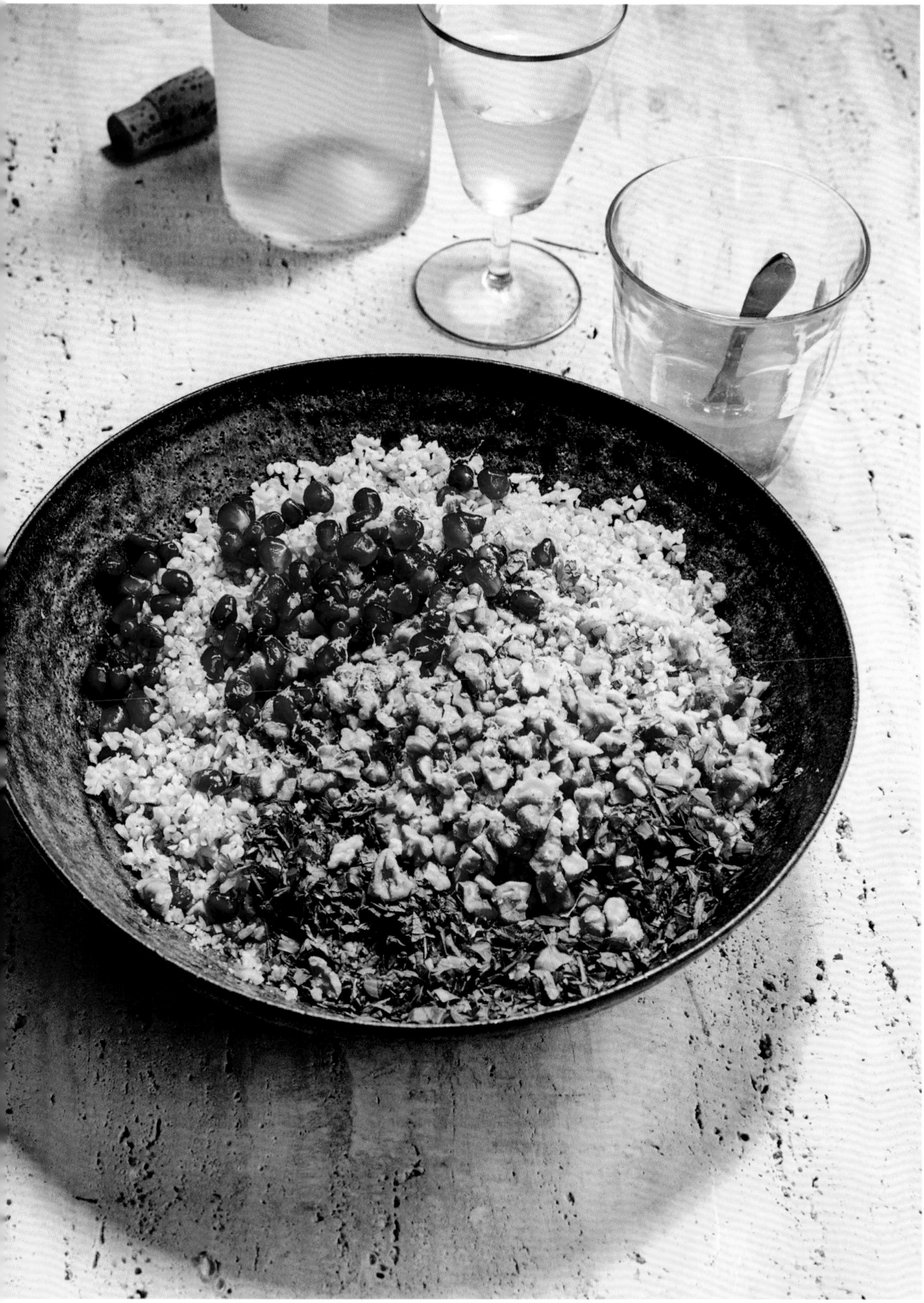

Brown Butter Couscous

Serves 6 to 8

Cooking couscous in browned butter that's nutty and aromatic is a simple way to elevate and intensify store-bought. Since we're not making our couscous by hand here, this is the perfect quick dish that's saved me in many last-minute dinner scrambles.

8 tablespoons (1 stick) unsalted butter

2 cups couscous

1 teaspoon kosher salt

Pinch of ground cinnamon

2½ cups boiling water or chicken or veg stock

In a medium pot, cook the butter over medium heat until it begins to smell nutty, about 5 minutes. Add the couscous, salt, and cinnamon, mixing thoroughly to work in all of the bits of brown butter from the bottom of the pot. Add the boiling water, stir, and remove from the heat. Cover the pot and let it stand for 5 minutes while the steam does the rest of the work. Fluff with a fork and serve hot.

Turmeric and Toasted Cumin Rice

Serves 4

Inspired by the rice that you usually get with your Indian feasts to sop up every drop of curry, this dish is the ideal playmate for just about any other recipe in this book. It's deeply fragrant and flavorful in a way that brings out the best qualities of any dish it's paired with. This dish is inspired by my time in India, but the flavors that you get when you steam cumin seeds with basmati rice is just so amazing and happens to go well with all the Middle Eastern flavors in this book.

1 cup basmati rice

1½ tablespoons grapeseed oil

1 teaspoon cumin seeds

½ teaspoon ground turmeric

1½ cups vegetable stock, chicken stock, or water

1 teaspoon kosher salt

1 In a sieve, rinse the rice under cool running water until the water runs clear.

2 In a medium pot, heat the oil over medium heat. Add the cumin seeds and toast just until fragrant, about 1 minute. Add the turmeric and the rice and stir to combine. Add the stock and salt, increase the heat to high, and bring the mixture to a boil. Reduce the heat to low, cover, and simmer for 12 minutes. Fluff with a fork and serve hot.

Persian Rice Tahdig

Serves 8

Tahdig (tah-deeg) is one of my earliest food memories. Persian friends of ours would invite us over for dinner from time to time, and the mother would make a big pan of this dish. The rice on the inside would be fluffy and buttery, but the grains around the edges were crunchified into perfect golden-brown perfection—and we'd all fight over those bites. When I started cooking professionally, tahdig was the first dish I wanted to learn how to make. You're basically building a rice "cake" (with layers of basmati rice, yogurt, and butter) laced with warm spices like cinnamon and saffron and dotted with tart barberries. It gets cooked in a tightly covered pan, where the steam cooks the rice while the outside crisps. Then it's turned upside down out of the pan onto a platter, where—if you've done your job right—the crispy outside bits hold the moist inside like a mold. It takes a little bravery, but don't try to be a hero: Use a nonstick pan.

¼ cup sugar (if using barberries)

1 cup dried whole barberries or dried cherries, finely chopped

2 cups basmati rice

2 tablespoons kosher salt

1 teaspoon saffron threads

2 tablespoons whole-milk yogurt (Greek or otherwise)

2 tablespoons grapeseed oil

Grated zest of 1 orange

½ teaspoon ground cinnamon

8 tablespoons (1 stick) unsalted butter, cubed

3 tablespoons pistachios, lightly toasted and roughly chopped, for garnish

1 If using barberries, combine the sugar and ¼ cup water in a small pot. Bring to a boil over medium-high heat, then reduce the heat to a simmer and cook just until the sugar dissolves, about 3 minutes. Add the barberries, stir to coat, and simmer while stirring for about 2 minutes. Transfer the fruit to a baking sheet to cool while you finish the tahdig. (If using dried cherries, skip this step and add them as is in step 6.)

2 In a sieve, rinse the rice under cool running water until the water almost runs clear.

3 In a large pot, combine 8 cups water and the salt. (You want to salt the water like you're making pasta—it's your one shot to season the rice itself.) Bring to a boil over medium-high heat. Add the rice and cook until al dente, 5 to 6 minutes. Drain the rice.

4 Meanwhile, mix the saffron into 1 cup very warm (but not hot) water. Let sit for at least 10 minutes to let the saffron release all of its flavor.

5 In a medium bowl, combine 1 cup of the cooked rice, the yogurt, grapeseed oil, and 2 tablespoons of the saffron water. Mix thoroughly.

(recipe continues)

6 Spread the rice-yogurt mixture evenly on the bottom of a 10-inch lidded nonstick pot. Sprinkle 1 cup of the remaining cooked rice on top, followed by 2 tablespoons of the barberries, a pinch of orange zest, and a pinch of cinnamon. Add another layer of rice and repeat with the barberries, orange zest, and cinnamon, reserving a couple tablespoons of the barberries for garnish. The rice will start to dome and look "pointy" in the middle—that's okay! Keep it that way. Finish by dotting the top with the butter and pour the rest of the saffron water all over the top.

7 Wrap the lid in a kitchen towel and secure it around the handle with a rubber band. (The towel will ensure that no steam can escape the pot.) Cover the pot and cook over low heat until the rice around the edges is golden and crispy (it's okay to peek under the lid!), 25 to 30 minutes. Be sure not to burn the bottom layer of rice, though you do want a nice crust on the bottom.

8 Remove the lid, invert a large serving plate over the pot, and carefully flip them over together. (If it sticks, no worries! Just scrape it out and run with it.) Sprinkle the tahdig with the reserved barberries and the pistachios and serve right away.

Freekeh-Celery Tabbouleh

Serves 4

I'm not gonna write a cookbook about Middle Eastern cooking and *not* include a tabbouleh, but this isn't your standard bulgur and parsley situation. That said, this version is still just as refreshing and tasty as the original, which happens to be one of Ido's favorite salads. Using freekeh instead of bulgur adds this meaty chew to the dish, plus freekeh's unique nutty flavor. But the biggest and most underrated update this classic gets is the addition of celery. I feel like I was reintroduced to celery as an adult, and it's come a long way from ants on a log. With its clean, fresh flavor and succulent, crisp texture, seriously, it's time to take another look at celery. I highly recommend you make a bunch of this salad to eat through the week. Every time you open the fridge, you'll be so happy it's there waiting for you.

2 cups cooked cracked freekeh (follow the package instructions)

2 cups chopped fresh parsley

2 cups chopped fresh dill

2 celery stalks, finely diced

¼ cup plus 2 tablespoons extra-virgin olive oil

Grated zest and juice of 1 lemon

1 teaspoon kosher salt

In a large bowl, mix together the freekeh, parsley, dill, and celery. Add the olive oil, lemon zest, lemon juice, and salt and mix once more to combine.

Date and Dill Rice

Serves 4

This is, without a doubt, one of my favorite hot grain dishes to serve with meals. The rice gets steamed with butter so it's perfectly glossy and fluffy, then finished so simply with dates and dill, whose green flecks are beautiful against the white rice. It's a fresh, aromatic accompaniment that makes almost any dish better.

1 cup basmati rice

2 tablespoons extra-virgin olive oil

2 tablespoons unsalted butter

1 medium yellow onion, finely chopped

2 garlic cloves, minced

2 teaspoons kosher salt

1½ cups chicken stock, vegetable stock, or water

1¼ cups chopped fresh dill

½ cup chopped Medjool dates

1 lemon

1 In a sieve, rinse the rice under cool running water until the water runs clear.

2 In a medium pot, heat the olive oil and butter over medium heat. Add the onion and cook until translucent, about 5 minutes. Add the garlic and salt and sauté for 1 more minute. Stir in the rice and stock, increase the heat to medium-high, and bring to a boil. Reduce the heat to low, cover, and cook until all the water has evaporated, about 12 minutes. Fluff with a fork, then fold in the dill, dates, and a squeeze of lemon juice. Serve hot.

Herbed Orange Kamut

Serves 4

Kamut is another name for Khorasan wheat, an ancient grain that's due for its moment. I really do think that it'll start popping up everywhere—I believe in you, Kamut! A big, fat grain that Ayv loves to eat one by one, it's got nutty flavor like freekeh and great texture owing to its larger size. You can sub it in for pretty much any other grain in this book, or use it to make this gorgeous dish with fresh oranges, herbs, and pistachios. It's the kind of salad you make to keep in your fridge for the week . . . then eat the whole bowl for lunch. If you have trouble finding Kamut, or you want to try this salad with another grain, it will work well with freekeh or barley.

1 cup Kamut, soaked overnight and drained

Kosher salt

1 orange

½ cup roughly chopped toasted pistachios

½ cup chopped fresh dill

¼ cup chopped fresh mint

¼ cup extra-virgin olive oil

½ large shallot, finely diced

2 teaspoons white wine vinegar

2 teaspoons honey

Juice of ½ lemon

Freshly ground black pepper

1 In a medium pot, combine the Kamut, 3 cups water, and 1 teaspoon salt. Bring to a boil over medium-high heat, reduce the heat to medium-low, and cook for 30 minutes, stirring occasionally. The Kamut should be cooked through but still a little al dente. Drain and transfer to a serving bowl to cool slightly.

2 Zest the orange and reserve the zest. Slice both ends off the orange, then carefully slice off the remaining peel and the white pith. Gently slice into the orange between the white membrane stripes to release the segments of fruit.

3 Fold the orange zest and segments, pistachios, dill, mint, olive oil, shallot, vinegar, honey, and lemon juice into the Kamut. Mix well and season to taste with salt and pepper. Mix again and serve.

Cracked Freekeh with Pomegranate, Walnuts, and Mint

Serves 6

I love this combination of flavors: the pomegranate molasses gives everything this tangy tartness, which plays off the deep nuttiness of freekeh and the walnuts. Plus, the fresh pomegranate seeds look like little jewels nestled in the mix. Serve as a side to roast chicken (see page 211) or pork chops (see page 218)—or if you're like me, sit down to a giant bowl of it for lunch and feel perfectly content.

3 cups cooked cracked freekeh (follow the package instructions)

1½ cups walnuts, toasted and finely chopped

½ cup pomegranate seeds

½ cup chopped fresh parsley

⅓ cup finely chopped fresh mint

Grated zest of 1 lemon

3 tablespoons extra-virgin olive oil

Juice of ½ lemon

1 teaspoon kosher salt

1 teaspoon honey

1 teaspoon pomegranate molasses

1   In a large bowl, combine the freekeh, walnuts, pomegranate seeds, parsley, mint, and lemon zest.

2   In a medium bowl, whisk together the olive oil, lemon juice, salt, honey, and pomegranate molasses. Pour the dressing over the salad and toss to coat.

Lemony Mejadra with Extra, Extra-Fried Shallots

Serves 6

Mejadra is a Middle Eastern comfort food that's a combination of lentils, rice, and onions. As simple as it sounds, it really is all about the onions here. They develop sultry, deep flavor as they cook down and caramelize, then fried shallots are added to the top for even more onion ring–type decadence. If you think you're putting too many onions in this dish, then you're doing it right. I love serving this with roasted tomatoes and Garlicky Tahini (page 37), but it's not necessary. It's a complete—and delicious—dish on its own.

1 cup French lentils, rinsed

Kosher salt

1 cup grapeseed oil

3 large shallots, sliced

3 tablespoons extra-virgin olive oil

2 large yellow onions, finely diced

Freshly ground black pepper

1 cup basmati rice

3 garlic cloves, finely chopped

1 teaspoon ground cumin

1 teaspoon ground turmeric

¼ teaspoon ground cinnamon

1 lemon, cut in half

Garlicky Tahini (optional; page 37)

Roasted tomatoes (optional; see page 194)

1 In a medium pot, combine the lentils, 2 cups water, and a generous pinch of salt. Bring to a boil over medium-high heat, reduce the heat to a simmer, and cook for 10 minutes. Drain and set aside.

2 In a medium skillet, heat the grapeseed oil over medium-high heat. Add the shallots and fry until golden and crispy, about 3 minutes. Using a slotted spoon, transfer the shallots to a plate lined with paper towels to drain.

3 In a large skillet, heat the olive oil over medium-high heat. Add the onions and season with salt and pepper. Cook, stirring occasionally, until the onions are golden and caramelized, about 15 minutes.

4 Meanwhile, in a sieve, rinse the basmati under cool running water until the water runs clear.

5 To the onions, add the garlic, cumin, turmeric, cinnamon, and a generous pinch of salt and cook for an additional minute or two, until fragrant. Add the lentils, rice, and 2 cups water. Bring to a boil. Reduce the heat, cover, and simmer for 10 minutes. Remove from the heat and fluff the mixture with a fork. Squeeze over half of the lemon and toss again.

6 Serve with the fried shallots on top, along with the garlicky tahini and tomatoes, if desired, and the remaining lemon half cut into wedges.

Gimme Some Sugah

If there's any chapter in this book that drives home the sense of play that I want you to feel when you look in your cabinet and your fridge, it's definitely this one.

While Middle Eastern flavors obviously influence a lot of my cooking, this book isn't necessarily about showing you how to make traditional recipes. It's more about exploring new ingredients and how you can then apply them to dishes that inspire a little nostalgia and a lot of feel-goods. So for this chapter, I wanted to have some fun with recipes that you'll definitely recognize—chocolate chip cookies, sheet cake, even Popsicles—and give them a twist with ingredients from your Middle Eastern pantry.

Just an FYI: I try to not make my desserts too sweet. I'm just not a fan of anything overly sugared-up, plus you can eat more that way. You can't eat three pieces of a super-sweet cheesecake, but if it's properly sweetened? You definitely can and not feel like a beast.

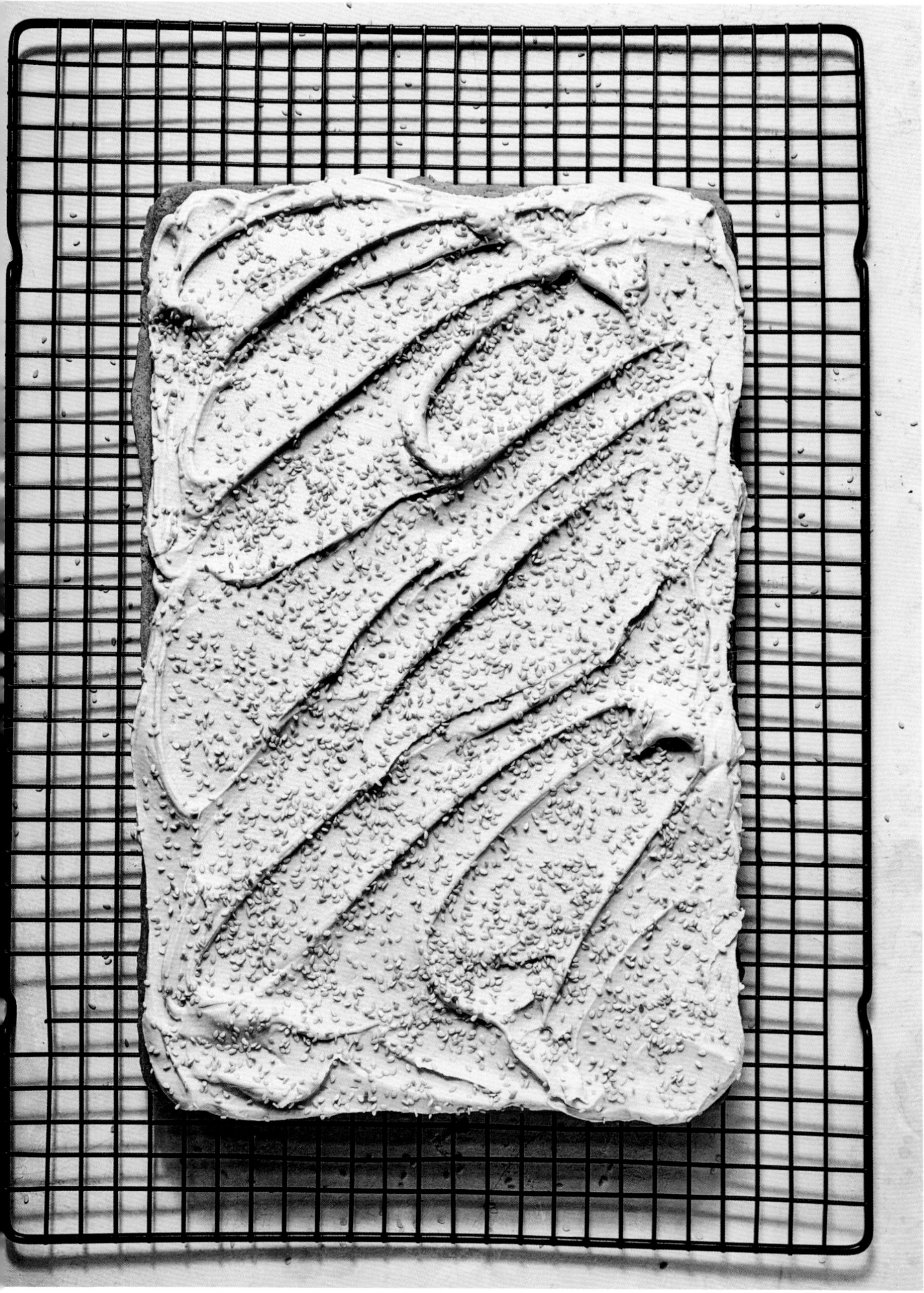

Salted Halvah Chocolate Chip Cookies

Makes 12 to 14 cookies

It's hard to improve on a chocolate chip cookie, but then I discovered that when you bake bits of halvah—a dense, flaky tahini confection—on top, it turns into caramelized marshmallow sesame heaven.

1⅓ cups all-purpose flour

¾ teaspoon baking soda

¼ teaspoon kosher salt

¼ teaspoon ground cinnamon

8 tablespoons (1 stick) salted butter, at room temperature

⅓ cup tahini paste

¾ cup packed dark brown sugar

¼ cup granulated sugar

1 large egg

1 teaspoon vanilla extract

1½ cups bittersweet chocolate chips

½ cup small chunks of halvah (see Note)

Flaky sea salt, for sprinkling

NOTE *If you can't find halvah, you can mix together 2 tablespoons of tahini with 2 tablespoons of honey. After you've flattened the cookies on the baking sheet, press small dents into each cookie and spread about a teaspoon of the mixture on each cookie. Finish with the sea salt.*

1 In a medium bowl, whisk together the flour, baking soda, kosher salt, and cinnamon. Set aside.

2 In a stand mixer fitted with the paddle attachment (or in a large bowl with a handheld mixer or a spoon), mix together the butter, tahini, brown sugar, and granulated sugar on medium-high speed until light and airy, about 5 minutes. Add the egg and vanilla and mix until well combined. Reduce the mixer speed to medium, add half the flour mixture, and mix to combine. Add the remaining flour mixture and mix to combine, scraping down the sides with a spatula, if necessary. Use a spoon or spatula to fold in the chocolate chips. Cover the bowl with plastic wrap and refrigerate the dough for at least 1 hour or overnight. (You can actually do this up to a week in advance!)

3 Preheat the oven to 325°F. Line two baking sheets with parchment paper.

4 Using your hands, roll a golf ball–size piece of dough into a ball for each cookie. Place the cookies about 2 inches apart on the prepared baking sheets and push down a little on each ball to flatten it slightly. Place a couple little pieces of halvah on top of each cookie and gently press them into the dough. Sprinkle with the sea salt.

5 Bake until the cookies are lightly golden, 12 to 15 minutes. Allow the cookies to cool slightly on the pan before transferring them to a cooling rack to cool completely. Store in an airtight container at room temperature for up to 1 week.

Yogurt and Sour Cream Cheesecake

Makes one 9-inch cake

Israeli-style cheesecake is lighter than the dense, thick versions that you usually get in the States and typically features a whipped sour cream topping, which gives the whole thing a bright, tangy flavor. When I was living in India and running a café there, I wanted to reinvent the concept a bit by adding yogurt, one of my favorite additions to cake because it brings creamy richness without weighing down the dessert. The result is a cheesecake that is Mediterranean-style light but satisfies even the most hardcore New York–style fans.

Graham Cracker Crust

15 graham crackers, ground in a blender or food processor (should equal about 2 cups)

8 tablespoons (1 stick) unsalted butter, melted

Pinch of kosher salt

Cheesecake Filling

1 (8-ounce) package cream cheese, left to soften at room temperature for at least 1 hour

1½ cups whole-milk Greek yogurt, at room temperature

⅔ cup granulated sugar

Pinch of kosher salt

1 teaspoon vanilla extract

3 large eggs, at room temperature

Whipped Sour Cream Topping

¾ cup heavy (whipping) cream

3 tablespoons powdered sugar

Grated zest of 1 lemon

¾ cup sour cream

NOTE *I love a chilled cheesecake, which is a great dessert for making a day ahead. Just keep it in the pan and wrap tightly with plastic wrap.*

1 **Make the graham cracker crust:** Preheat the oven to 325°F.

2 In a medium bowl, mix together the graham cracker crumbs, melted butter, and salt. Press half of the mixture into the bottom of a 9-inch springform pan in an even layer. Set aside the other half of the crust mixture.

3 Bake the crust until toasted and lightly golden, 5 minutes. Let the crust cool completely before adding the filling. (Leave the oven on.)

4 **Make the cheesecake filling:** In a stand mixer fitted with the paddle attachment (or in a large bowl with a handheld mixer or a spoon), whip the cream cheese until airy, about 1 minute. Beat in the yogurt, granulated sugar, salt, and vanilla until smooth, about 5 minutes, making sure the cream cheese is fully incorporated. Add the eggs one at a time, fully mixed in each before adding the next.

5 Use a rubber spatula to press the cream cheese mixture through a sieve directly into the graham cracker crust. (This will help get rid of any cream cheese lumps.) Gently tap the sides of the pan to release any air bubbles. Bake until the filling has set, 30 to 35 minutes. Let the cake cool completely in the pan while you make the topping.

6 **Make the whipped sour cream topping:** In a stand mixer fitted with the whisk attachment (or in a large bowl using a handheld mixer or a whisk), combine the heavy cream, powdered sugar, and lemon zest and whip on medium-high speed until the cream is at soft peaks, 3 to 5 minutes. Add the sour cream and whip once more until just combined (make sure to not overmix the whipped cream here or you'll end up with butter). If needed, you can cover and refrigerate the topping until the cheesecake has fully cooled (or for up to 3 days).

7 Evenly spread the topping over the cooled cheesecake and sprinkle over the reserved graham cracker crumbs. You could serve the cake now, but I highly recommend chilling it in the fridge or even the freezer before serving.

Baklava Crostata

Crust

1½ cups all-purpose flour

1 tablespoon granulated sugar

½ teaspoon kosher salt

8 tablespoons (1 stick) unsalted butter, cut into chunks and very cold

¼ cup ice-cold water, plus a little extra if needed

Filling

2 cups walnuts or pistachios, toasted

4 tablespoons (½ stick) unsalted butter, melted

3 tablespoons granulated sugar

2 tablespoons heavy cream

Grated zest of 1 lemon

½ teaspoon kosher salt

¾ teaspoon ground cinnamon

¼ teaspoon ground cloves

¼ teaspoon ground cardamom

Finishing and Serving

All-purpose flour, for dusting

1½ cups plus 2 tablespoons heavy (whipping) cream

2 teaspoons Demerara or granulated sugar, for sprinkling

¼ cup granulated sugar

1 tablespoon fresh lemon juice

NOTE: *This is just as lovely for breakfast as it is for dessert.*

Makes one 12-inch crostata or two 6-inch crostatas

Baklava is one of the most quintessential Middle Eastern desserts. It's extremely sweet, rich, and gooey—so much so that you usually can't have more than a bite or two. I wanted to take the same ingredients but lighten the whole thing up. I swapped the fussy phyllo dough for a flaky crostata shell, filled it with the traditional walnut and spice mixture, glazed it with a lemony syrup, and topped it off with unsweetened whipped cream. Same flavors, less work, and more food in my belly.

1 **Make the crust:** In a food processor, combine the flour, granulated sugar, and salt. Pulse a few times to combine. Add the butter and pulse until the mixture reaches a sandy texture. Add the ice water a few teaspoons at a time, pulsing until the mixture just holds together. You may not need the full ¼ cup water, or you might need a teaspoon or two more.

2 Turn out the dough onto plastic wrap and shape it into a ½-inch-thick disk. Wrap the disk tightly and refrigerate for 1 hour.

3 Preheat the oven to 350°F. Line two baking sheets with parchment paper.

4 **Make the filling:** In a food processor, finely chop the toasted walnuts. Be sure to keep an eye on them or they'll turn to butter. In a medium bowl, combine the walnuts, melted butter, granulated sugar, cream, lemon zest, salt, cinnamon, cloves, and cardamom. Mix thoroughly and set aside.

5 **To finish and serve:** Remove the dough from the plastic wrap. Sprinkle a little flour on the work surface and, if making 2 smaller crostatas, divide the dough evenly in half. Roll out the dough into a ¼-inch-thick round and transfer the crust to a baking sheet (two sheets if making 2 crostatas). Spoon the filling over the center of the dough, leaving about a ½-inch border around the edges. Lightly brush the edges with water and fold the edges over the filling (this can be imperfect and rustic!). Lightly brush the exposed crust with 2 tablespoons of the cream and sprinkle with the Demerara sugar. Bake until the crust is lightly golden, about 40 minutes.

6 Meanwhile, combine the granulated sugar and ¼ cup water in a small saucepan. Bring to a simmer over medium heat and let the sugar dissolve, about 3 minutes. Continue simmering until the simple syrup reduces slightly, another minute. Remove the pot from the heat and stir in the lemon juice. When the crostata comes out of the oven, brush the simple syrup over the top of the filling.

7 Whip the remaining 1½ cups cream to soft peaks and serve with the crostata.

Sumac-Strawberry Mini Pavlovas with Vanilla Whipped Cream

Makes 10 mini Pavlovas

The first time I had a Pavlova, I was working at an Australian restaurant in London while studying at Le Cordon Bleu. I fell in love with these delicate clouds topped with vibrantly colorful fruit, and for someone who isn't nuts about too-sweet desserts, it's always been a favorite. I wanted to come up with a unique twist and settled on strawberries and sumac, which are a gorgeous pair—the sumac's citrus notes fold right into the sweetness of the berries. The Pavlovas are also relatively simple to make; you just have to have time on your side as the meringues bake at a low temperature and then cool completely while still in the oven, which dries them out. The lower the temp, the less color you get, which is what you want.

Pavlovas

5 large egg whites

Pinch of kosher salt

1 cup sugar

1 teaspoon vanilla extract

1 teaspoon almond extract (optional)

1 tablespoon cornstarch

1 teaspoon distilled white vinegar

Sumac Strawberries

3 cups thinly sliced strawberries

2 tablespoons sugar

Grated zest of 1 lemon

Juice of ½ lemon

1 teaspoon sumac, plus more for serving

Vanilla Whipped Cream

2 cups heavy (whipping) cream, kept very cold

Grated zest of 1 lemon

Seeds from 1 vanilla bean

1 Make the Pavlovas: Preheat the oven to 250°F. Line a baking sheet with a silicone baking mat or parchment paper.

2 In a stand mixer fitted with the whisk attachment (or in a large bowl using a handheld mixer or a whisk), whip the egg whites and salt on high speed until the egg whites begin to look fluffy, about 5 minutes. With the mixer running, begin adding the sugar 1 or 2 tablespoons at a time. Once all the sugar is added, continue mixing until the mixture is thick and glossy, 5 to 10 minutes. Add the vanilla and almond extract (if using) and mix until just combined. Reduce the speed to low, sprinkle in the cornstarch and vinegar, and mix for just a few seconds to combine.

3 Using a silicone spatula or a metal offset spatula, place 10 roughly even dollops of the meringue on the prepared baking sheet. Spread them out slightly, so they're about 3 inches in diameter, leaving a slight dip in the middle to hold the fruit and whipped cream.

4 Place the baking sheet in the oven and immediately reduce the heat to 225°F. Bake for 1 hour; the meringue should be barely crisp on the outside and still soft inside. Turn off the oven and leave the Pavlovas inside until the oven is completely cool, at least 2 hours. (You can even let them sit in the oven overnight.) The Pavlovas can be stored in an airtight container at room temperature for up to 3 days.

(recipe continues)

5 **Make the sumac strawberries:** In a medium bowl, combine the strawberries, sugar, lemon zest, lemon juice, and sumac. Mix to coat the strawberries, cover, and let macerate in the refrigerator for at least 30 minutes and up to 1 hour.

6 **Make the vanilla whipped cream:** In a stand mixer fitted with the whisk attachment (or in a large bowl using a handheld mixer or a whisk), whip the cream on high speed until it begins to thicken, about 3 minutes. Add the lemon zest and vanilla seeds and continue whipping until the cream forms soft peaks, 3 more minutes. If you find you've overwhipped the cream and it's gotten lumpy, add a splash of fresh cream and mix on medium speed until the mixture loosens a bit.

7 **To serve:** Fill each meringue with ¼ cup whipped cream followed by 3 tablespoons of the macerated strawberries. Sprinkle with a tiny pinch of sumac and serve.

Tahini Sheet Cake

Makes one 9 × 13-inch cake

When you get on the tahini train, it's hard not trying to find a way to use it in every recipe you make. Lucky for us, when it comes to dessert, it's a natural fit. I tried whipping it into a buttercream and the result is In. Sane. It adds creamy body while tempering the richness of the frosting, and the lemon-scented cake brightens the pairing. You've probably had a million sheet cakes before, but never one like this.

Cake

½ cup (1 stick) unsalted butter, at room temperature, plus more for the pan

3½ cups all-purpose flour, plus more for the pan

2 teaspoons baking powder

1½ teaspoons kosher salt

1 teaspoon baking soda

½ cup grapeseed, sunflower, or safflower oil

1¾ cups granulated sugar

4 large eggs, at room temperature

1 cup whole milk, at room temperature

½ cup tahini paste, at room temperature

2 teaspoons vanilla extract

Grated zest of 2 lemons

1 cup sour cream, at room temperature

Buttercream

2 sticks (8 ounces) unsalted butter, at room temperature

2 cups powdered sugar

½ cup tahini paste, at room temperature

1 teaspoon vanilla extract

½ teaspoon kosher salt

Serving

2 tablespoons toasted sesame seeds, for garnish

1 **Make the cake:** Preheat the oven to 350°F. Butter and flour a 9 × 13-inch baking pan.

2 In a medium bowl, whisk together the flour, baking powder, salt, and baking soda. Set aside.

3 In a stand mixer fitted with the paddle attachment (or in a large bowl with a handheld mixer or a spoon), cream the butter on medium-high speed until light and fluffy, about 2 minutes. Add the oil and granulated sugar and continue to whip it until light and fluffy, about another 2 minutes, scraping down the sides with a spatula as needed. Add the eggs one at a time, waiting until each egg is incorporated before adding the next. Beat in the milk, tahini, vanilla, and lemon zest. Add the sour cream and mix just until it's incorporated, only a few seconds.

4 Reduce the speed to low (this helps keep the flour from whooshing up in the mixer) and add half of the flour mixture to the butter mixture, increasing the speed to medium as more flour gets incorporated. Repeat with the other half of the flour mixture and mix for about 1 minute, just until it all comes together.

5 Pour the batter into the prepared pan, using a spatula to help smooth it evenly. To help the batter settle evenly in the pan, gently lift the pan an inch or two off the work surface and drop it back down. Repeat a couple of times.

6 Bake until a skewer or cake tester inserted into the center comes out clean, about 30 minutes. Let the cake cool completely in the pan while you make the frosting. You could also invert the cake onto a cooling rack after allowing it to cool in the pan for about 10 minutes, then serve it on a platter or tray.

(recipe continues)

7 Make the buttercream: In a stand mixer fitted with the paddle attachment (or in a large bowl with a handheld mixer or a spoon), cream the butter on medium-high speed until light and fluffy, about 2 minutes. Add the powdered sugar and continue mixing until well combined, making sure to scrape down the sides. Add the tahini, vanilla, and salt and continue mixing until the mixture is light and fluffy, about 5 minutes. The frosting will be nice and thick.

8 To serve: Liberally frost the cake with the buttercream and sprinkle with the sesame seeds.

NOTE *You can make the frosting up to 2 days in advance and store it in the fridge. Just be sure to let the frosting sit at room temp for about 20 minutes to soften before spreading it over the cake.*

Semolina, Olive Oil, and Honey Cake with Cherries

Makes one 9-inch cake

This cake is sort of a mash-up between a *basbousa* (a Middle Eastern semolina cake) and the classic Mediterranean olive oil cake. It's a refreshingly simple dessert with clean, subtle fruity notes from the oil (you'll want to use a good one here) and a floral flavor. You can top it with just about anything. Cherries are my first choice, and figs, pomegranate, and apricots would be lovely, too, but go with whatever looks good at the market.

Honey-Lemon Glaze

⅓ cup granulated sugar

2 tablespoons honey

Juice of ½ lemon (about 1 tablespoon)

Olive Oil Cake

Unsalted butter for the pan

1¼ cups all-purpose flour, plus more for the pan

1 cup semolina flour

1¼ cups granulated sugar

1 teaspoon baking powder

1¼ teaspoons kosher salt

½ teaspoon baking soda

3 large eggs

¾ cup plain whole milk yogurt

½ cup whole milk

1 cup extra-virgin olive oil

¼ cup honey

Grated zest of 1 lemon

Grated zest of 1 orange

Whipped Yogurt

1 cup heavy (whipping) cream

¾ cup plain Greek yogurt

2 tablespoons powdered sugar

1 scant teaspoon vanilla extract

Serving

Powdered sugar, for dusting

1 cup pitted cherries or other seasonal fruit

1 Make the honey-lemon glaze: In a small saucepan, combine the granulated sugar, honey, and ⅓ cup water and bring to a boil. When the sugar is dissolved, remove from the heat and add in the lemon juice.

2 Make the olive oil cake: Preheat the oven to 350°F. Butter and flour a 9-inch round nonstick cake pan.

3 In a medium bowl, whisk together the semolina flour, all-purpose flour, granulated sugar, baking powder, salt, and baking soda. In a large bowl, whisk together the eggs, yogurt, milk, olive oil, honey, and lemon and orange zests. Add the flour mixture to the wet ingredients, whisking thoroughly to combine.

4 Pour the batter into the prepared pan. Bake until a knife or cake tester comes out clean, 45 to 50 minutes. Brush with the glaze and let the cake cool for at least 20 minutes in the pan before serving.

5 Make the whipped yogurt: In a stand mixer fitted with the whisk attachment (or in a large bowl using a handheld mixer or a whisk), whip the cream on medium-high speed until it reaches soft peaks, about 5 minutes. Add the Greek yogurt, powdered sugar, and vanilla and whip again until the mixture is light and fluffy, 1 to 2 minutes.

6 To serve: Lightly dust the cake with powdered sugar. Serve with the whipped yogurt and cherries (or other seasonal fruit).

NOTE *This cake can get pretty brown on top. To prevent this from happening, cover the top of the pan with foil halfway through baking.*

Mint-Lemonade Pops

These are inspired by one of my favorite Israeli summertime drinks, *limonana*. It's lemonade, mint, and ice blended into a slushie that's perfect for steamy afternoons. If you wanted to, you could just skip the ice pops and serve this as a drink—splash of vodka, arak, or tequila optional. (Just don't add it to the pops themselves or they won't freeze!)

½ cup sugar

1 cup fresh lemon juice
(from about 8 lemons)

⅓ cup packed fresh
mint leaves

Shot or two of arak, vodka,
or tequila (if not freezing
as pops) (optional)

1 In a medium saucepan, heat ½ cup water over medium heat until quite warm (but not boiling) and stir in the sugar. Mix until the sugar is dissolved, 1 to 2 minutes. Let this simple syrup mixture cool completely.

2 In a blender, combine the simple syrup, lemon juice, mint leaves, alcohol (if using), and 1 cup water. Blend until the mint is broken down into fine flecks.

3 Pour the liquid into 4 to 6 ice pop molds, depending on their size, distributing it equally. Freeze until completely frozen and set, at least 4 hours. Or serve as is over ice if you've added alcohol.

Acknowledgments

I have been obsessed with cookbooks since my stoner days in high school, and publishing my own has always seemed like this big, crazy, seemingly unattainable dream. So I'm having a real "pinch me" moment writing these acknowledgments. I'm humbled to think that it's now my turn to share my food and my stories with people who will be making these recipes for their families. It's a dream come true, and I couldn't have done it without any of these incredible people:

Let's start with Jennifer Sit, the most badass editor babe Clarkson Potter has ever *seen*. Thank you, thank you, THANK YOU for believing in me, encouraging me, and pushing me. You've given me the greatest gift: confidence. And because of you, this book is more special than I could have imagined. Thank you for holding my hand!

My agent, Eve Atterman. Your guidance throughout this process has been invaluable. Your unwavering support and zero-judgment approach allowed me to ask all the dumb questions and to have the confidence to build the best team imaginable. Your understanding and support of my vision and food made me so excited to write this book.

My collaborator, Rachel Holtzman. From the first conversation we had, I knew we'd be instant friends. Your honesty and humor made it easy for me to open up and tell my story exactly the way I wanted to, and I couldn't ask for anything more. Thank you for being an incredible sounding board, for your patience, and for keeping me on track—the hardest job of all!

Aubrie Pick, you're not just a photographer, you're an *artiste*. Watching you work was truly a magical experience. Thank you for pushing me where I needed to be pushed, for turning the set into a collaborative space, and for bringing my vision to life. I will always treasure our work together.

Kalen Kaminski, I love your style and taste so much that I literally took the pants right off of your body for this shoot. You gave the book that coolness factor that I knew you would. Please style my life and home, okay? Thanks! ;)

Chelsea Zimmer, you are a fucking badass! Your food styling is so on-point, and it makes a pretty killer combo with your warmth and sense of humor. You understood exactly what I was trying to do the second you walked through my door, and I could not be more thankful.

Gordan Sawyer, thank you for the endless laughs. You were such a dream to work with.

Cathryn Greenwald, thank you for all the grocery store trips, epic playlists, and great laughs. You have been not only a great assistant and recipe developer/tester but also a great friend. I'm so lucky that we found each other when we did (over IG, no less!).

The amazing team at Clarkson Potter: Stephanie Huntwork, Patricia Shaw, Heather Williamson, Laura Palese, Andrea Portanova, Stephanie Davis, and Erica Gelbard—thank you for helping me raise this book baby with such tender love and care. It wouldn't be nearly as beautiful, polished, and special without you.

Randi Brookman Harris, I absolutely love working with you. Your aesthetic is gorgeous, your positivity is infectious, and I love our friendship. Thank you for always coming through.

Ido, my best friend, my biggest cheerleader. Thank you for your endless patience and constant positivity. You are my ray of sunshine . . . every single day. I cherish our relationship more than anything in this world. I knew the recipes were complete and ready for the book when I could envision us eating them together in the kitchen with our hands and a bottle of wine, and in our sweats. I couldn't have done any of this without you. You are my home. My life.

My parents: Mom, Dad, what can I say? You have been the best parents any kid could ask for. Your unwavering support and encouragement have brought me to this place. You have given me the ability to explore and understand who I am and the path that I needed to take, which was definitely the one less traveled. Your guidance, creativity, and understanding of who I am and what I needed growing up has been a huge part of my success and how I have gotten to this place. Thank you for showing me the world and helping me learn just how much I'm capable of. I love you.

Arielle and Renny, my crazy, funny, wild sisters. You are my best friends and my creative partners in life. Thank you for pushing me to be the fullest expression of me. And thank you for making me laugh so hard that I cry and cry so hard that I laugh. I'm so lucky that I get to dance and sing around the table with you for the rest of my life. I love you forever.

Emma Hacohen, we were always meant to be in each other's lives. Growing up in Toronto together, then living together in Israel and then New York City, you were there since the beginning of it all. Thank you for letting me send you every single image from this book and for helping me make decisions about style and design. But mostly, thank you for being there for me when I need you.

Lindsay Nicholson, we have been on such a mind-blowing incredible life journey and I can't tell you how much it has meant having you by my side to listen to me vent, stress, laugh, and cry for so many years. You really manage to show up when I need you the most. You are also such a badass in the kitchen and I value your opinion and palate. Your confidence in me and my food has given me the confidence I needed to put out this book. I love you.

Index